HOW TO PLAY

BAWU

AND

HULUSI

A BEGINNER'S GUIDE
TO THESE POPULAR
CHINESE WIND INSTRUMENTS

BY

PAT MISSIN

www.patmissin.com

HOW TO PLAY BAWU AND HULUSI:
A Beginner's Guide To These Popular Chinese Wind Instruments

Copyright © 2011 by Patrick R. Missin

All rights reserved. No part of this book may be reproduced in any form, or by any electronic or mechanical means, including information storage and retrieval systems, without the express permission of the author. The only exception is by a reviewer, who may quote short excerpts in a review.

All traditional tunes presented in this book are believed to be in the public domain. If this is not the case, please contact the author so that future editions may be ammended appropriately.

Printed in the United States of America

First printing 2011

ISBN-10: 1467912980

ISBN-13: 978-1467912983

www.createspace.com

CONTENTS

INTRODUCTION 6

BUYING A BAWU OR HULUSI 7

ABOUT THE BAWU 10

ANATOMY OF THE BAWU 12

ABOUT THE HULUSI 13

ANATOMY OF THE HULUSI 15

ABOUT THE NOTATION USED IN THIS BOOK 16

BAWU BASIC PLAYING TECHNIQUE 18
    Getting Your First Note 18
    Playing The Basic Scale 19
    Some Common Problems 20

HULUSI BASIC PLAYING TECHNIQUE 22
    Getting Your First Note 22
    Playing The Basic Scale 23
    Some Common Problems 24

ADDITIONAL PLAYING TECHNIQUES 26
    Articulation 26
    Vibrato 27
    Portamento 28
    Ornamentation 29
    Underblowing 31
    Half Holing 31
    Cross Fingering 33
    Playing In Other Keys 34

FAMILIAR WESTERN TUNES ... 40
- Amazing Grace ... 42
- Auld Lang Syne ... 44
- London Bridge ... 46
- Scarborough Fair ... 48
- El Condor Pasa ... 50

TRADITIONAL CHINESE TUNES ... 51
- Golden Peacock Jumps Lightly ... 56
- Song Of Yimeng Mountain ... 57
- Lady Meng Jiang ... 58
- Love Song Of Kang Ding ... 59
- Embroidering The Pouch ... 60
- Miao Minority Song ... 62
- When The Moon Rises ... 63
- The Terraces ... 64
- Lusheng Dance ... 66
- Luquan Folk song ... 68
- The Little Flowing Stream ... 69
- Midu Folk Song ... 70

CARE AND MAINTENANCE ... 71
- General Care ... 71
- Reed Care And Adjustment ... 72
- Tuning ... 74

NONSTANDARD INSTRUMENTS ... 75
- Double Instruments ... 75
- Unusual Drone Notes ... 75
- Keys And Double Fingerholes ... 76
- Additional Fingerholes ... 76

READING JIANPU NOTATION ... 78
- Pitch ... 78
- Timing ... 78
- Rests ... 79
- Other Symbols ... 79
- Amazing Grace ... 80

FINGERING CHARTS 81
    Key Of Low D 81
    Key Of F 81
    Key Of G 81
    Key Of A 82
    Key Of B♭ 82
    Key Of C 82
    Key Of High D 82

RECOMMENDED LISTENING 83

FURTHER INFORMATION 85

INTRODUCTION

Interest in the music and musical instruments of other cultures is not something new. Marin Mersenne's 1636 book "Harmonie Universelle" featured several non-European instruments, the composer Claude Debussy was greatly influenced by the Javanese gamelan music he heard at the Paris World Exhibition of 1889 and in the 1960s, musicians like Ravi Shankar rose to international superstar status. However, with the growth of the Internet, it is now easier than ever to obtain recordings and musical instruments from all over the world. By logging on to a site like eBay, anyone can buy authentic South American panpipes, African percussion, obscure stringed instruments from India and CDs of virtuoso musicians playing in every conceivable style of music.

Two instruments that have become particularly popular in recent years are the bawu and hulusi. These are both free reed instruments originating in South West China. However, unlike the more well known free reed instruments such as the Chinese sheng, Laotian khaen and the Western accordion and harmonica, all of which have a separate reed for each note, both the bawu and hulusi use a single free reed connected to a flute-like bamboo tube with fingerholes. They produce a beautiful evocative tone that has been used quite frequently in movie soundtracks, including the international hit "Crouching Tiger, Hidden Dragon". They are relatively easy to learn and the basic techniques are the same for both instruments, but until now, there has not been a dedicated instruction book for them in the English language. I can't promise that this book will turn you into a virtuoso overnight, but it contains more than enough to get you off to a good solid start.

BUYING A BAWU OR HULUSI

If you haven't already got yourself a bawu or hulusi, then a few pointers on buying one might be in order. Even if you already have one, there is a good chance that you will be buying another at some point.

If you live in or travel through China or neighbouring countries, or you have an eclectically stocked musical instrument store near you, then you may be able to buy one in person. If you already have the basic playing skills, you can ask the vendor to let you try an instrument to get an idea how well it plays. If you don't have those skills yet, you may be able to ask the vendor to demonstrate it for you. However, you may want to bear in mind that if the vendor is happy to let you play it, then there's a good chance that yours is not the first mouth that has been on that mouthpiece. How much this bothers you depends on your own attitudes towards hygiene issues. I'm not a doctor, but I doubt there is any real risk of transmitting an infection after the instrument has been allowed to air out fully, although you probably don't want to exchanging fresh saliva with someone you wouldn't feel happy kissing. It's your call.

If you are not in Asia, then you are probably most likely to be buying your bawu or hulusi via mail order. If possible, ask for a picture of the instrument before buying. Stress that you want to see the actual one you are considering, not one that is "just like it". As the brass reeds used in these instruments are somewhat fragile, you will still need to place some trust in the dealer, though, so make sure that they have a good returns policy. Unlike fine violins, hulusi and bawu do not really improve with age, so I would advise against purchasing a used instrument, unless you are feeling particularly lucky.

Examine the instrument as best you can, looking for any cracks and splits. It doesn't take much to have an adverse affect on the performance of a wind instrument and a small crack in a material like gourd or bamboo can soon turn into a disaster area after a few changes in humidity. Also keep an eye open for small holes the size of pin pricks, especially if you notice any fine sawdust falling from the open ends of the bamboo. There are a wide variety of woodworm-like critters in Southwest China and you really don't want to import one of them into your home! Try to get an idea of the quality of the workmanship. Obviously, if it looks like something that your niece made as a kindergarten craft project, then the chances are good that it might not play that well either. On the other hand, don't confuse fanciness with good workmanship - the best hulusi I own is a rather plain looking instrument, but extremely well put together. If the instrument does not come with a case, see if you can get one included for a nominal fee, especially if you are having the instrument sent to you via international mail.

You shouldn't have to pay a lot of money for a decent quality instrument. They are made in China (and more recently, Vietnamese-made hulusi are appearing on the market) and the price will reflect the lower wages over there, although they will also reflect the cost of shipping them to your part of the world if you do not live in China. At the time of writing, you really shouldn't need to spend more than US$100 to get a good quality instrument and US$200 should buy you something very special. On the other hand, beware of extremely cheap instruments. A lot of relatively obscure instruments from around the world are made in cheap versions designed to be hung on a tourist's wall, rather than played. I've also noticed a tendency for some Chinese dealers on eBay to advertise an instrument for a ridiculously low price, like 99c, but then charge $100 or more for shipping. I would encourage you not to support that kind of marketing, especially if they will only refund the cost of the instrument if there is a problem, but not the cost of the shipping. Above all, don't rush into buying anything - these instruments are much more readily available now than they were just a few years ago, so you can afford to bide your time and get a good deal.

A wide variety of materials are used in the construction of the bawu and hulusi - which you prefer for your own instrument is a matter of personal choice. Traditionally bamboo has been the usual material, with a bottle gourd used for the windchest of the hulusi. More recently turned wood has been used, rosewood and ebony being particularly popular, as well as instruments constructed entirely from various plastics. The latter have an obvious advantage if you live somewhere prone to dramatic changes in humidity, but the materials themselves have much less effect on the tone of the instrument than other factors, so pick what appeals most to you.

Like harmonicas and pennywhistles, hulusi and bawu are made in various keys. Usually the key is stamped between the third and fourth fingerholes of the instrument. C and Bb are the most common keys for the hulusi, with G and F being the most common keys for bawu, but other keyed instruments can be obtained. This book is written assuming that you have an instrument in either C or G. If you have one in a different key then you can still play the tunes in this book, they will just come out at a different pitch. If you intend to play along with recordings or other musicians, then you will probably want to pick up instruments in various other keys at some point.

ABOUT THE BAWU

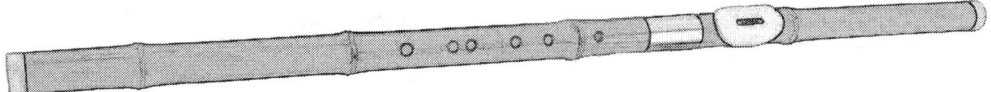

The bawu is a side-blown reedpipe found in Southern China, played by the Dai, Hani, Miao (Hmong), Yi and other minorities. When in use it resembles a typical side-blown bamboo flute, but the sound is produced by a triangular free reed made from brass set into the side of the pipe. The reed is surrounded by a mouthpiece, traditionally made of bone, but these days commonly made of plastic.

The traditional bawu has six fingerholes and one thumbhole, giving a range of a little more than an octave and is most commonly found in the keys of G and F. The key is designated by the pitch that is produced with the thumbhole and the three uppermost fingerholes closed, so a bawu in the key of G produces the basic scale D E F# G A B D E. Additional pitches can be played by underblowing, cross fingering and/or half holing and a G instrument would typically also be played in the keys of D, C and sometimes A and Bb, along with their relative minor keys. Most bawu are made from two sections and the overall tuning of the instrument can be varied by adjusting the joint between the two pieces.

In recent years, the rich, mellow tone of the bawu has become a favorite with composers of film soundtracks and many small Chinese music ensembles now feature a bawu player. "Improved" bawu have appeared over the last few decades, with added drones, increased range, moisture-resistant synthetic materials, finger keys, etc. One of the most common variations on the traditional design is the double bawu which consists of a pair of bawu in different keys joined together so that their mouthpieces are in close proximity, allowing the player to switch quickly between them to play in a higher or lower register.

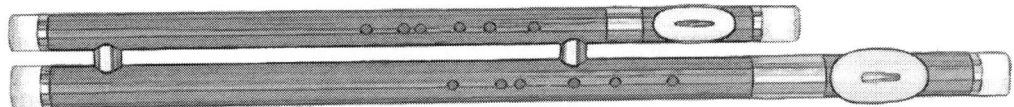

Another common variation is the vertical bawu. These have a small windchest and are played in the upright position, resembling a simplified hulusi.

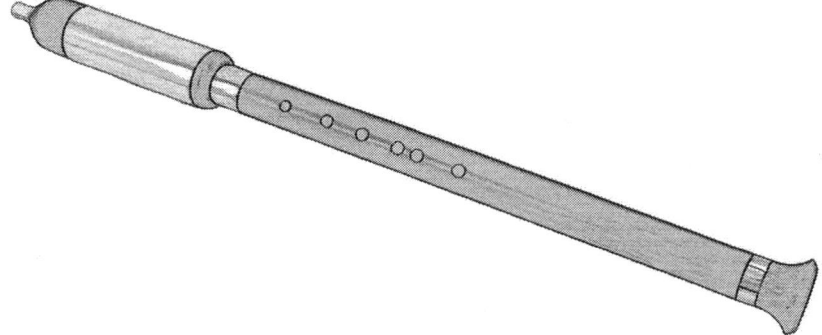

For the purposes of instruction, we will assume that your bawu is pitched in G. If it is in a different key, the playing technique will be identical, but the notes will simply be of a higher or lower pitch than the music notation shows. In the back of this book there are charts showing the notes produced by bawu in different keys.

ANATOMY OF THE BAWU

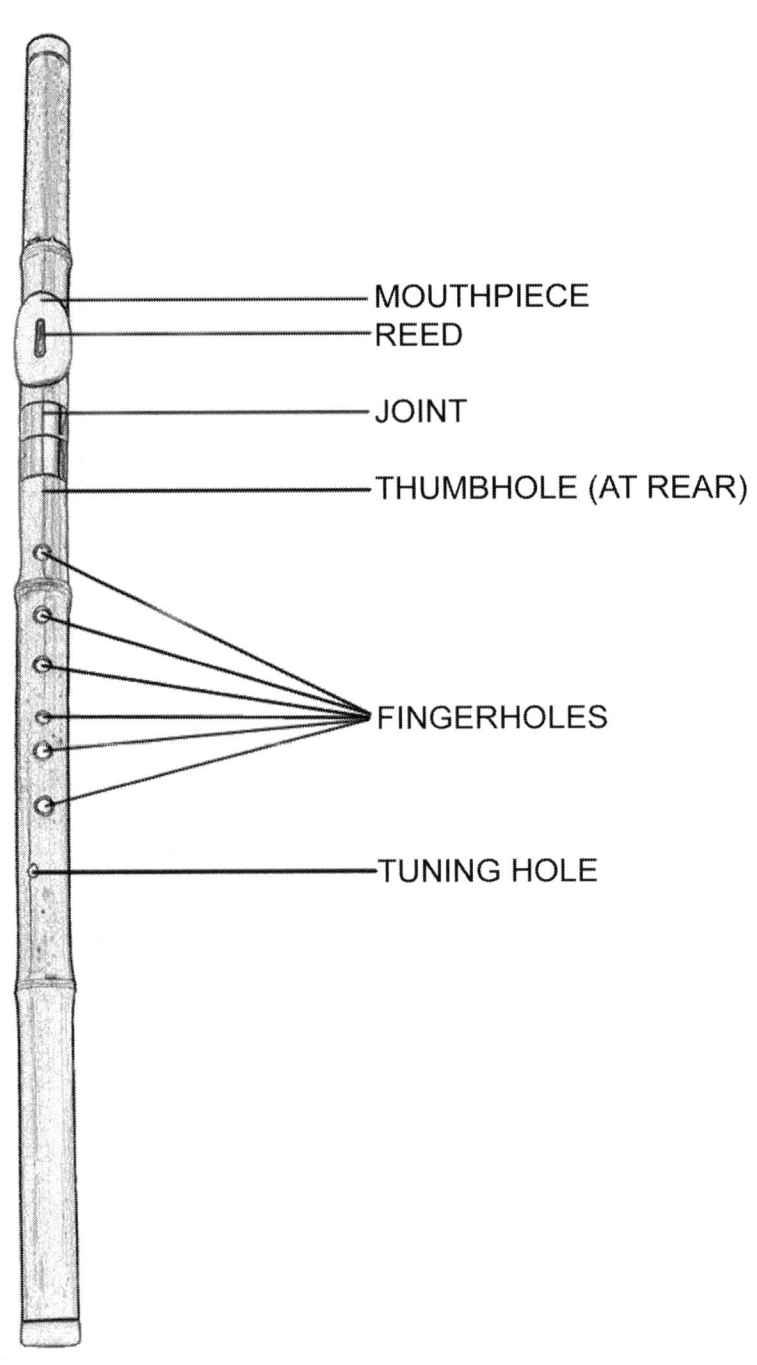

ABOUT THE HULUSI

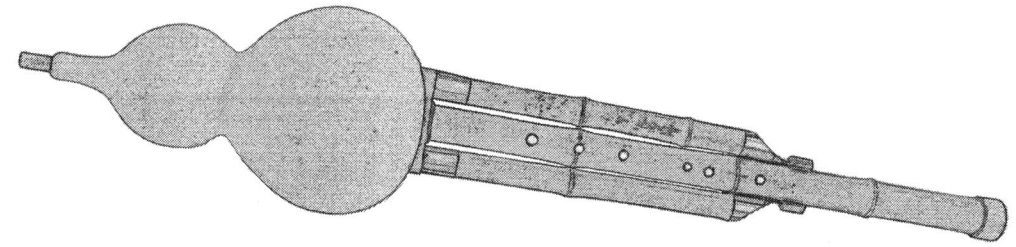

The hulusi (which means "gourd silk", referring to the instrument's silky tone), also known as the huluxiao (translating roughly as "gourd flute"), is an end-blown free reed pipe with a gourd windchest. Visually, it somewhat resembles the Indian snake-charmer's flute, although it is completely unrelated. Single pipe specimens are rare, most hulusi having a melody pipe and at least one drone pipe. The most common version has a melody pipe and two smaller pipes, one supplying the drone, the other a dummy pipe added for visual symmetry.

The hulusi is most commonly associated with the Dai minority (who call it bilangdao), but it is also found amongst other minority groups of Southern China such as the Achang (who call it paileweng), De'ang (who have versions called wogebao and milun), Wa (who have versions called baihongliao and beiban) and others. Each sounding pipe has a triangular free reed made of brass and the fingering of the melody pipe is that same as that of the bawu.

The most common keys are C and Bb, although the hulusi is usually available in a much wider range of keys than the bawu. As with the bawu, the key of the instrument is designated by the note that is produced with the thumbhole and the three uppermost fingerholes closed, so a C hulusi plays the scale G A B C D E G A. Like the bawu, additional melodic pitches can be played by underblowing, cross fingering and half holing.

The drone pipe of a C hulusi usually plays a high E and if a second drone is present, it usually plays a low A. The drone(s) can be switched off, traditionally by plugging the end of the pipe, although newer models have often have fingerholes or keys to control the drone. As with many traditional instruments of the Chinese ethnic minorities, "improved" versions have been produced, with increased melodic range and metal, plastic or ceramic replacements for the gourd windchest. So-called double hulusi have also been developed, with two melody pipes that can be either be played independently for greater melodic range, or simultaneously for polyphonic playing. There are also several recently developed hybrid instruments that combine features of both the bawu and the hulusi, such as the buluo and the benti.

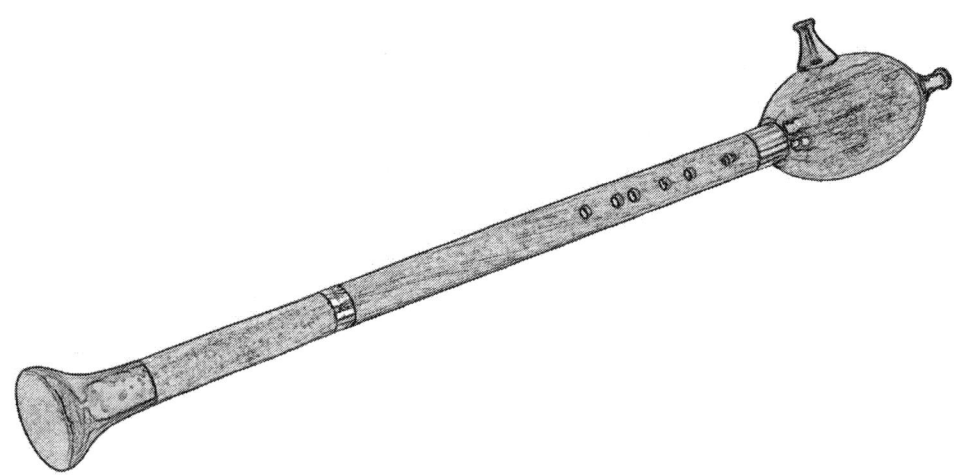

As with the bawu, the hulusi's popularity has increased dramatically over the last few years, both in China and the rest of the world and it is often featured in movie soundtracks and CDs of New Age music.

For the purposes of instruction, we will assume that your hulusi is pitched in C. If it is in a different key, the playing technique will be identical, but the notes will simply be of a higher or lower pitch than the music notation shows. In the back of this book there are charts showing the notes produced by hulusi in different keys.

ANATOMY OF THE HULUSI

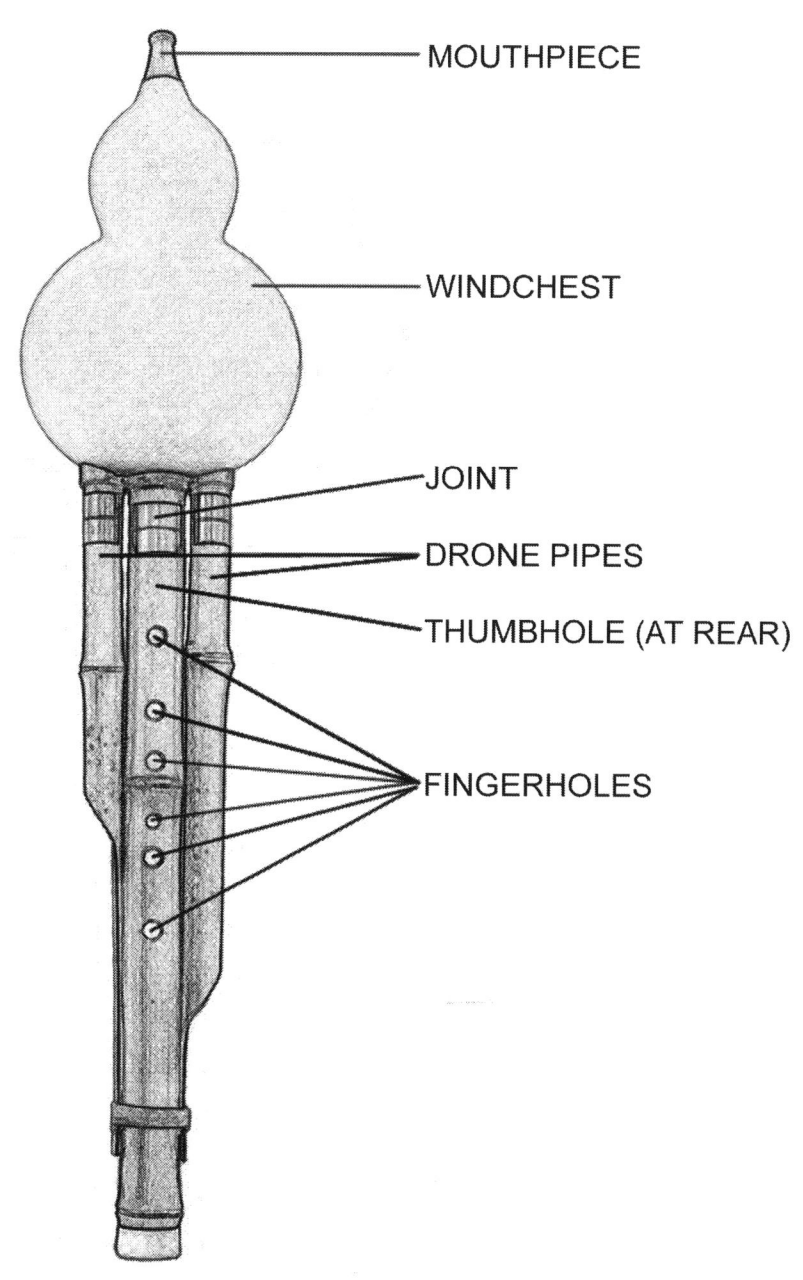

ABOUT THE NOTATION USED IN THIS BOOK

The tunes and musical examples presented in this book use standard Western musical notation and, in some cases, a form of tablature. Standard notation describes the notes that are to be played; tablature describes where those notes are located on the instrument. Although tablature (often called "tab" for short) is most commonly associated with nonclassical instruments, especially fretted stringed instruments like the guitar, it has a long history of use dating back several hundred years and various forms of tab exist for almost every instrument.

As the bawu and hulusi have identical fingering, we will be using the same tab for both of them. Underneath each note on the standard staff will be placed a symbol to show the fingering for that particular note. The symbol consists of an upright column with seven small circles - the upper circle represents the thumbhole; the next three circles represent the upper three fingerholes and the lower three circles represent the lower three fingerholes. An empty circle indicates that that particular hole is to be opened; a filled in circle indicates that it is to be closed. A half closed circle indicates that the hole should be partially closed - more on this in the chapter on additional playing techniques.

It is usually assumed that the left hand is going to play the thumbhole and upper three fingerholes, with the right hand being used to play the lower fingerholes. Most Western woodwind instruments are similarly played with the left hand in the upper position. If you are one of the 10% of the population who is left handed, or if you are right handed, but feel more comfortable with your right hand in the upper position, then please feel free to do whatever works best for you. If you do decide to do it the other way around, then keep in mind that when I say "left hand" you should use your right hand and when I "right hand" you should use your left hand - right? One thing to keep in mind, however, is that if you later acquire a bawu or hulusi with keys or doubled fingerholes you may need to change back to the "normal" position to play them. It's your call.

Some recently made hulusi (and perhaps some bawu, although I have not seen any examples) come with double fingerholes in some positions, usually with a sort of scooped out shape in the pipe wall with one larger hole and one smaller hole close together. Again, this will be covered in a little more detail in the chapter on additional techniques, but in the meantime treat the pair of them as a single hole to be closed with a single finger.

It may be worth adding that if you have any missing digits, please use whatever feels most comfortable for you and whatever closes off the appropriate holes in the most efficient way. Remember, the goal here is not to develop conservatory-standard musicianship, but to have fun playing music. When in doubt, keep a close eye on the tablature and you can't go too far wrong!

The tab used in this book does not indicate the timing or the duration of the notes, merely what fingering is used to play them. If you don't read standard notation, you can download recorded examples of the exercises and tunes in this book to hear how they should sound.

Examples in standard notation will always be written with the key signature of the instrument on which it is to be played. Examples for a C instrument will be written using the key signature of C major (i.e.. no sharps and flats), regardless of the key of the piece of music itself. Likewise, example for a G instrument will use the key signature of G major (a single sharp).

Ini additional to tab and standard notation, some things will be explained using solfège, the familiar *do re mi* syllables. To help distinguish these from the surrounding text, they will be in italics and if the examples feature the same note in different octaves, the lower octave notes will be capitalised. We will be using what is called "movable do solfège", where do always indicates the first note of the major scale in whatever key were are in. For example, in the key of C, *do re mi fa so la ti* will represent C D E F G A B; in the key of G it will represent G A B C D E F#; in the key of Bb it will represent Bb C D Eb F G A; in the key of F it will represent F G A Bb C D E; etc. Again, don't get too bogged down in this stuff right now. It will all start to make sense once you begin making music.

BAWU BASIC PLAYING TECHNIQUE

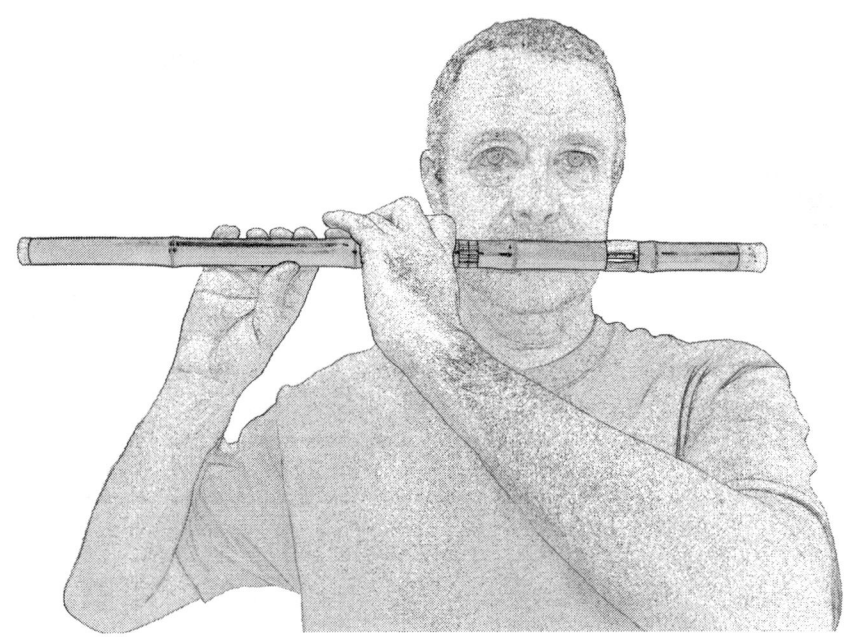

GETTING YOUR FIRST NOTE

The toughest part of learning any wind instrument is usually getting that first clear note, so let me guide you through the process step by step. This chapter assumes that you have a traditional transversely-played bawu. If you have an upright bawu, please follow the instructions in the hulusi chapter.

Sit with the bawu resting loosely in your lap, with the mouthpiece towards your left. Locate the thumb hole at the rear of the instrument and place your left thumb over it. Now place your left index finger over the fingerhole nearest the bawu's joint, your left middle finger over the next fingerhole and your left ring finger over the third fingerhole. Next, place your right index finger over the fourth fingerhole, your right middle finger over the fifth fingerhole and your right ring finger over the last fingerhole. Most traditional bawu have one more additional hole beyond the sixth fingerhole, but this is for the purpose of tuning the lowest note of the instrument and does not need any of your fingers on it (often this is placed to the side or rear of the pipe).

Keeping the bawu horizontal, raise it so that the mouthpiece comes up to meet your mouth. You may need to twist the upper section of the bawu slightly to bring the mouthpiece into a more comfortable position. Relax your lips and place them against the bawu, surrounding the mouthpiece completely so that no air can escape. Make sure that your fingers are completely closing all the fingerholes and blow softly. You should hear a somewhat muted low pitched tone. Now tense your lips slightly and blow a little harder and that note should leap up in pitch and the tone should become a little crisper. Practise alternating between these two notes for a while. The difference in pitch between these two notes should be a minor third - think of the first notes of the Brahms lullaby. If any of the pitches are unstable, check to make sure your fingers are closing off the fingerholes properly. The lower of these two notes is an underblown note; the higher one is the lowest "normal" note of the bawu - try practising hitting this note cleanly without sounding the underblown note first. Once you are reasonably comfortable with this, we can move on to play the basic scale of the bawu.

PLAYING THE BASIC SCALE

With all the fingerholes closed, play the "normal" note (ie, not the underblown one), then lift off your fingers in turn from each fingerhole - start by lifting your right ring finger, right middle finger, right index finger, left ring finger, left middle finger, left index finger and finally lift your left thumb from the thumb hole, leaving all the holes completely open. At this point, the bawu should be supported mostly by the thumb and little finger of your right hand, possibly using the edge of your left index finger to keep the mouthpiece pushed firmly against your mouth. You will find that you need to increase the air pressure slightly for each note as you ascend the scale. You will also probably notice that the tone of each note is slightly different - oboe-like in the lower register and more like a clarinet in the upper register. This is perfectly normal.

If your bawu is in the key of G, here are the notes of the basic scale you just played:

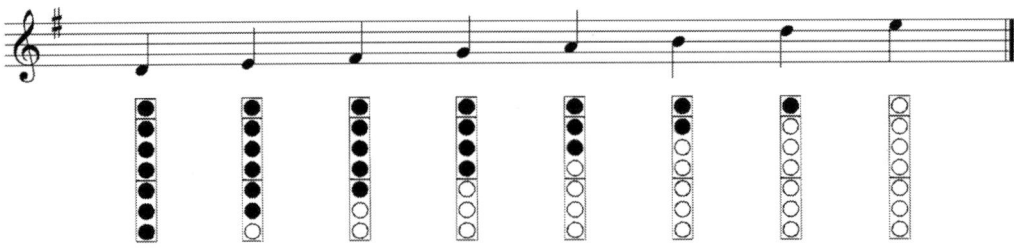

In solfège, these would be the notes *SO, LA, TI, do, re, mi, so* and *la*.

To descend the basic scale, simply start with all the holes open, then close them off one by one, starting with the left thumb and finishing with the right ring finger. Practise running up and down this scale for a while. Try doing it with one long breath to form a string of connected notes, then try using individual breaths to sound a series of separated notes. Practice the scale at different speeds, practice playing long notes and short notes - use your imagination to find different ways to play this basic scale until it becomes second nature and your fingers fall into place for each note without really having to think about it.

SOME COMMON PROBLEMS

As with most musical instruments, in the early stages of practice, you are likely to make a few strange noises along the way. Most often this will be due to your fingers not fully closing off the appropriate fingerholes and/or not sustaining a nice even breath pressure. After a while, the fingering should start to feel more natural and the muscles of your fingers will get stronger. Likewise, as you practise you will get better at judging the correct air pressure required for each note. A very common problem is caused by starting the note with insufficient breath pressure, causing the underblown note to sound for a short while before the intended note kicks in. A related problem is a slight squawking noise at the end of a note. Lower notes are more prone to this problem than higher ones, but it is caused by not cutting off the airstream cleanly at the end of the note, allowing the reed to sound an underblown pitch. You can try quickly opening your mouth just a little at the end of the note to release the extra air pressure, or you can cut off the airstream sharply with your tongue, but take care not to catch the tip of your tongue with the tip of the reed!

HULUSI BASIC PLAYING TECHNIQUE

GETTING YOUR FIRST NOTE

The hulusi is played in a very similar manner to the bawu, the main difference being that it is played in a vertical position. To start out, it's a good idea to switch off the drone pipe or pipes. Traditional models often have a small foam plug attached by a thread to the lower end of the drone pipe. If yours has one of these and it is not inserted into the end of the drone pipe, do so now. If the drone pipe has a fingerhole, place your little finger over it - left little finger for the left pipe, right little finger for the right pipe. If the drone has a spring loaded key, flip it so that it is closed.

Stand or sit with the hulusi in front of you, with the mouthpiece pointing upwards. Locate the thumb hole at the rear of the instrument and place your left thumb over it. Now place your left index finger over the uppermost fingerhole, your left middle finger over the next fingerhole and your left ring finger over the third fingerhole. Next, place your right index finger over the fourth fingerhole, your right middle finger over the fifth fingerhole and your right ring finger over the last fingerhole. Many hulusi have one more additional hole beyond the sixth fingerhole, but this is for the purpose of tuning the lowest note of the instrument and does not need any of your fingers on it (often this is placed to the side or rear of the pipe).

Raise the hulusi so that the mouthpiece comes up to meet your mouth. Relax your lips and place them around the mouthpiece, making sure to get a good seal so that no air can escape. Make sure that your fingers are completely closing all the fingerholes and blow softly. You should hear a somewhat muted low pitched tone. Now tense your lips slightly and blow a little harder and that note should leap up in pitch and the tone should become a little crisper. Practise alternating between these two notes for a while. As with the bawu, the difference in pitch between these two notes should be a minor third (the opening notes of the Brahms lullaby again). If any of the pitches are unstable, or you are hearing a cluster of notes, check to make sure you fingers are closing off the fingerholes properly and that the drones are switched off. The lower of these two notes is an underblown note; the higher one is the lowest "normal" note of the hulusi - try practising hitting this note cleanly without sounding the underblown note first. Once you are reasonably comfortable with this, we can move on to play the basic scale of the hulusi.

PLAYING THE BASIC SCALE

With all the fingerholes closed, play the "normal" note (ie, not the underblown one), then lift off your fingers in turn from each fingerhole - start by lifting your right ring finger, right middle finger, right index finger, left ring finger, left middle finger, left index finger and finally lift your left thumb from the thumb hole, leaving all the holes completely open. At this point, the hulusi should be supported mostly by the thumb and little finger of your right hand, possibly with your left little finger helping to stablise it. You will find that you need to increase the air pressure slightly for each note as you ascend the scale. You will also probably notice that the tone of each note is slightly different - oboe-like in the lower register and more like a clarinet in the upper register. This is perfectly normal.

If your hulusi is in the key of C, here are the notes of the basic scale you just played:

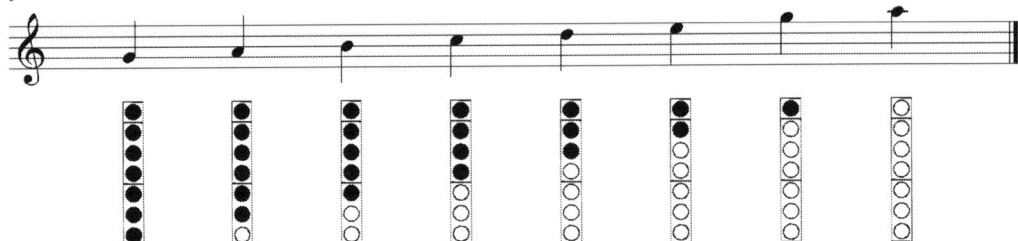

In solfege, these would be the notes *SO*, *LA*, *TI*, *do*, *re*, *mi*, *so* and *la*.

To go back down the scale, simply start with all the holes open, then close them off one by one, starting with the left thumb and finishing with the right ring finger. Practise running up and down this scale for a while. Try doing it with one long breath to form a string of connected notes, then try using individual breaths to sound a series of crisply separated notes. Practice the scale at different speeds, practice playing long notes and short notes - use your imagination to find different ways to play this basic scale until it becomes second nature and your fingers fall into place for each note without really having to think about it.

SOME COMMON PROBLEMS

As with most musical instruments, in the early stages of practice, you are likely to make a few strange noises along the way. Assuming that you have switched off the drone pipes, then most of the time, those strange noises will probably be due to your fingers not fully closing off the appropriate fingerholes. After a while, the fingering should start to feel more natural and the muscles of your fingers will get stronger.

Likewise, as you practise you will get better at judging the correct air pressure required for each note. A very common problem is caused by starting the note with insufficient breath pressure, causing the underblown note to sound for a short while before the intended note kicks in. A related problem is a slight squawking noise at the end of a note. Some instruments are more prone to this than others and it is usually more of an issue with lower notes than with higher ones, but it is caused by failing to cut off the airstream cleanly at the end of the note, allowing the reed to sound an underblown pitch. You can cut off the airstream sharply by touching your tongue to the mouthpiece, or by quickly opening your mouth just a little at the end of the note to release the extra air pressure.

ADDITIONAL PLAYING TECHNIQUES

ARTICULATION

Articulation is the technical term for how musicians shape the notes that they play. Sometimes you may want to start a note as softly as possible and slowly increase your breath pressure until the note reaches its full volume. Or you may want to play a flowing series of notes that are all sounded with one single breath - this is described by the Italian word legato. At other times you might want each note to be crisply separated from the adjacent notes - this is known as staccato and is usually achieved on wind instruments by tonguing. This is done by starting the note with your tongue briefly touching either the mouthpiece of the instrument or the roof of your mouth, as though you are saying "ta" or "tuh" (but doing it silently) so that the airflow starts suddenly and crisply, giving a sharp attack to the note. The same technique can also be used to cut off a note sharply, which helps prevent that accidental sounding of the underblown note, as described in the basic techniques section.

Double-tonguing is used to articulate a faster series of notes and is done by silently saying "ta-ka" or "tuh-kuh" for each pair of notes. Triple-tonguing is used to articulate notes in groups of three, using "ta-ka-ta" or "tuh-kuh-tuh".

T T T T   T K T K T K T K   T K T T K T T K T

A word of warning if you are playing a traditional bawu: be careful not to catch the tip of the reed with the tip of your tongue - the tip of the reed is very sharp and can easily draw blood. It is also quite easy to damage the reed or knock it out of correct adjustment.

VIBRATO

Vibrato is the pulsing variation in pitch used to add expression to vocals and to instrumental music. With most wind instruments, it is achieved by modulating the airflow by rhythmic contractions of the abdominal muscles, upper respiratory tract, vocal chords and/or embouchure. Developing a good vibrato technique on trumpet, clarinet, saxophone, or whatever, can take a lot of time and effort, but on the bawu and hulusi it is much easier.

Let's start by playing the keynote (*do*) of your instrument, with the thumbhole and three left hand fingerholes closed. Now take the middle finger of your right hand and slowly move it towards the second right hand fingerhole, but don't completely close that fingerhole. As your finger nears the fingerhole you should hear the note start to lower in pitch; move it away from the fingerhole and the pitch will rise again. In order to produce vibrato you simply repeat this process. The closer your finger gets to the open fingerhole, the more intense the vibrato effect and the faster you do it, the faster the vibrato.

Now let's try adding vibrato to the second note of the scale (*re*), played by closing the thumbhole and upper two finger holes. Take the index finger of your right hand and move it back and forth above the highest right hand fingerhole. Next play the third note of the scale (*mi*) by closing the thumbhole and highest fingerhole and moving the third finger of your left hand back and forth above the third fingerhole. Try adding vibrato to each of the other notes of the scale in a similar fashion. With the low sixth (*LA*) of the scale (played by closing all except the lowest fingerhole) you will have to produce the vibrato by moving your third right hand finger over the lowest fingerhole. This sort of vibrato can only be added to the lowest "normal" note (*SO*) if your instrument has a tuning hole that you can reach with the little finger of your right hand. You can also obtain a vibrato-like effect by rhythmically increasing and decreasing your breath pressure.

Vibrato is most often notated by a wavy line above the note.

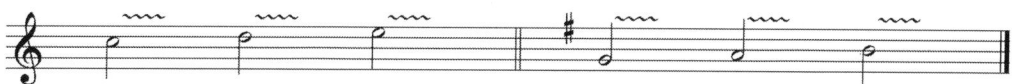

PORTAMENTO

Portamento is the Italian term for a gradual slide from one note to another and this is one of the most distinctive effects used on both the bawu and the hulusi. Let's start by playing the low *LA* note, with the thumbhole, left hand fingerholes and upper two right hand fingerholes all closed. If you just lift your middle finger from the second right hand fingerhole, the note will jump from *LA* to *TI* However, if instead you gradually remove your finger to uncover the hole bit by bit, then the pitch will glide gradually from *LA* to *TI*. If you then gradually remove your index finger from the uppermost right hand fingerhole, the note will slide up to *do*.

Now go back to playing the low *LA* note, but this time gradually lift your right index and middle fingers at the same time and the pitch will glide smoothly all the way up to do. Even wider gliding effects are possible. Play the low *LA* note again, but this time raise your right index and middle fingers AND your left middle and ring fingers, causing the note to glide all the way up from *LA* to *mi*. Practice sliding between all the notes on your instrument, both up and down and at different speeds. It may take a little practice to get all of the different possible slides perfectly smooth, but it is well worth the effort.

Examples of portamento on a C instrument:

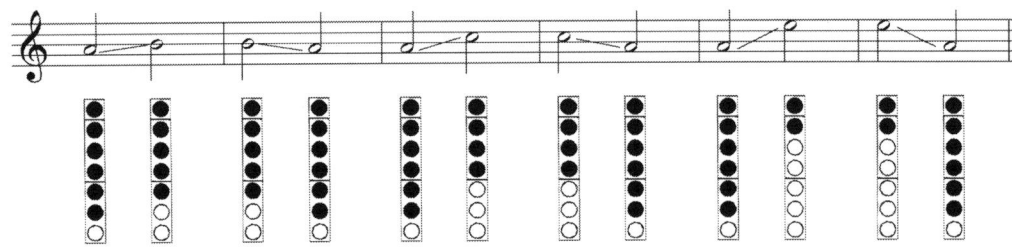

Examples of portamento on a G instrument:

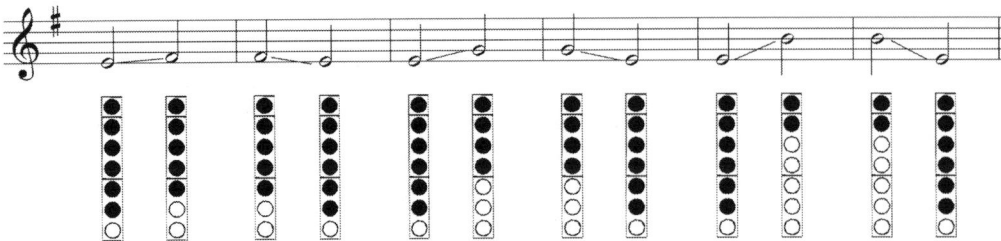

ORNAMENTATION

Ornamentation refers the various additional notes that are added to the basic melody to make a piece of music sound more interesting or personalised. Entire books have been written on the subject of ornamentation in various styles of music, but here we will deal with the ornaments most commonly used on the bawu and hulusi.

The most common ornament is probably the simple grace note. This is a note that is sounded very briefly before a main melodic note and is represented in Western notation by a smaller note symbol than is used for the other notes, often with a slash through the stem. Sometimes multiple grace notes precede the main note, the precise duration of the grace note(s) being left to the discretion of the player and regional stylistic preferences.

Examples of grace notes on a C instrument:

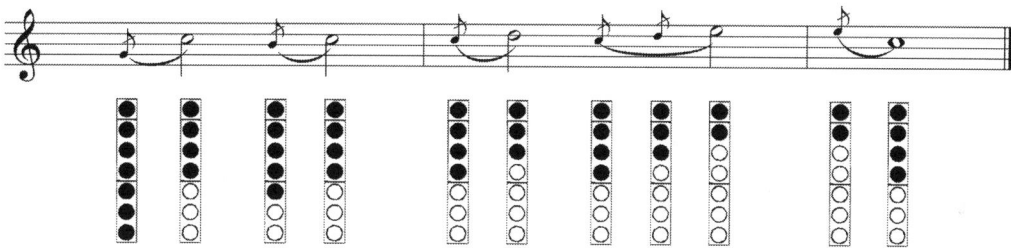

Examples of grace notes on a G instrument:

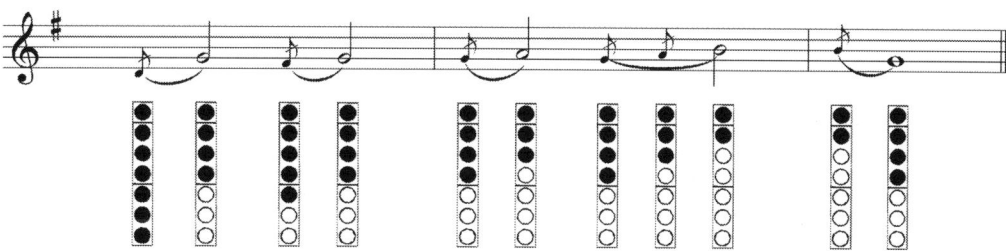

A fast alternation between the main note and its upper or lower neighbour is called a mordent. The upper mordent is indicated by the symbol ∾ and the lower mordent by the symbol ∾.

Examples of upper and lower mordents, as written and as played, on a C instrument:

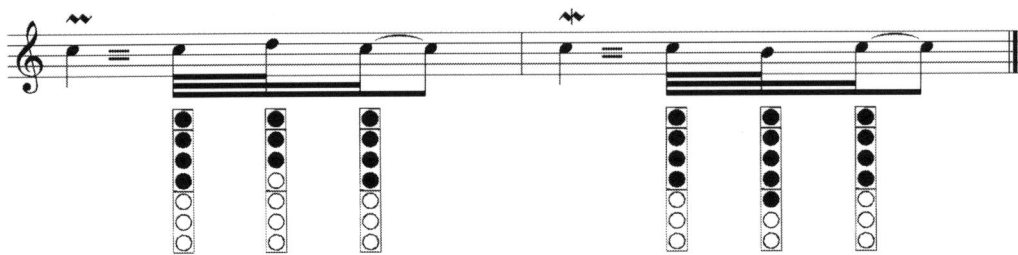

Examples of upper and lower mordents, as written and as played, on a G instrument:

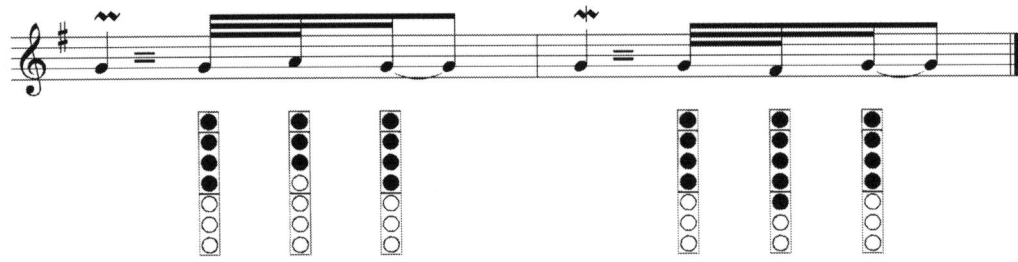

A repeated alternation between two notes is called a trill or shake and is usually indicated by *tr* above the note to be trilled. The speed and number of repetitions can vary quite a bit.

Examples of a trill, as written and as played, first on a C instrument then on a G instrument:

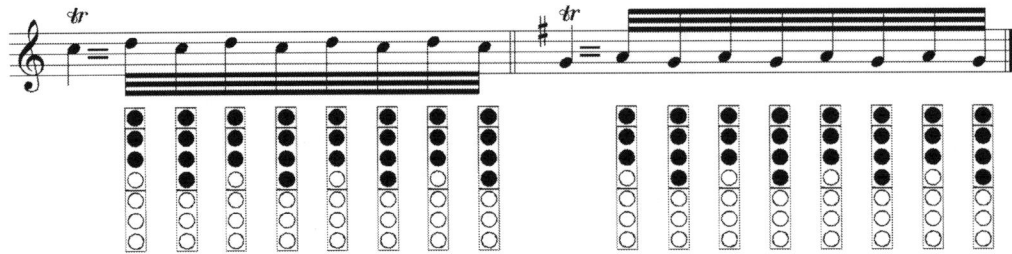

UNDERBLOWING

Remember when you were learning to get that very first note out of the instrument that there are two different notes available with all the fingerholes closed? The lower of those two notes, the one played with very soft air pressure, is called an underblown tone and is sometimes useful in its own right. We'll cover that a little later, but in the meantime practice moving between the underblown tone and the "normal" lowest tone. In the following examples, the underblown tone is indicated by an asterisk (*) above the note.

Examples of underblowing on a C instrument and a G instrument:

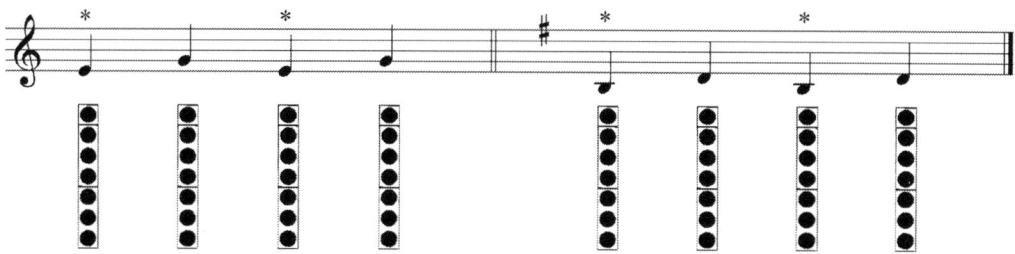

HALF HOLING

You have may have noticed that there are several notes missing from the basic scale of the bawu and hulusi. Not only are there no sharps or flats, the fourth note (*fa*) of the home scale is absent. There are a couple of ways to fill in the gaps, allowing a complete chromatic scale to be played. The first one is called half holing and the basic idea is to play the note immediately above the "missing" note, then partially cover the uppermost open hole to lower the pitch to the note you want. For example, in order to play that missing fourth note (*fa*), play the fifth (*so*) by closing just the thumbhole, then partially cover the highest fingerhole with your left index finger. Actually, this is probably the trickiest of all of the half holed notes, as there are actually two notes in between the third (*mi*) and the fifth (*so*) - as well as the fourth (*fa*) there is also the sharp fourth, alternatively known as the flat fifth (*fi* or *se* respectively in chromatic solfège). It takes a reasonably good ear to be able to hear where the half holed notes are supposed to be, but checking the notes against another instrument can help with the learning process. Alternatively, you could pick up a reasonably priced digital tuner from a music store (make sure you get a chromatic tuner, rather than one specifically for guitar), or there are also a lot of freeware computer programs available on the Internet that do the same thing.

Here is a complete chromatic scale using half holing on a C instrument:

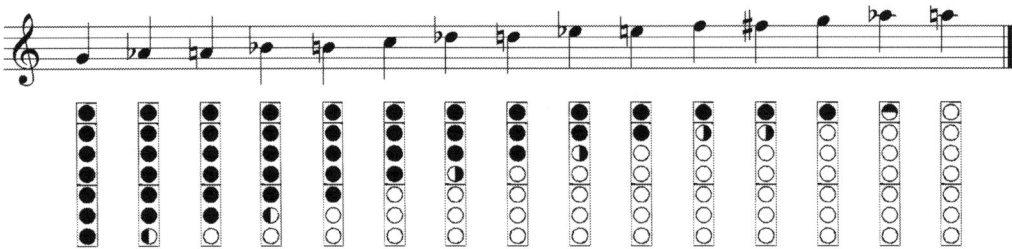

Here is a complete chromatic scale using half holing on a G instrument:

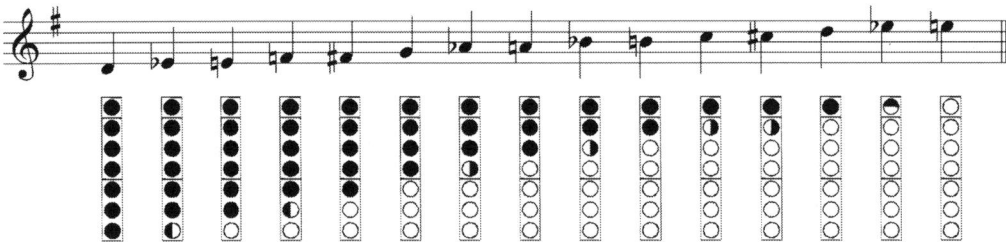

It is also possible to combine half holing with underblowing to play additional notes below the lowest normal note of the instrument, but this can be very challenging. Some instruments come with finger keys to allow these underblown notes to be played more easily and accurately.

The fourth note of the major scale is not of great importance to much of the music traditionally associated with the bawu and hulusi, but in order to make the instruments more easily applied to a wider range of musics, some manufacturers have recently made modifications that allow that note to be more easily played. One of the most common is the use of a double fingerhole operated by the left index finger. When other notes are played these fingerholes are opened or closed together as a pair, but to play the fourth note (*fa*) you close the thumbhole and cover just one of the pair of holes with your left index finger. Some instruments have a finger key for the fourth note. Usually the third of the scale (*mi*) is sounded as usual with the thumbhole and highest fingerhole closed, the fourth is sounded by pushing the key and the fifth (*so*) is sounded by opening the highest fingerhole and keeping the thumbhole closed. If your instrument has additional double fingerholes or keys, hopefully it came with a fingering chart.

CROSS FINGERING

Cross fingering is another way to get those "missing" notes on the bawu and hulusi. The tone produced by cross fingered notes is sometimes said to be inferior to that produced by half holing, but good intonation of the notes is usually considerably easier with cross fingering. The basic idea of cross fingering is to play the note immediately above the "missing" note, leave the uppermost of the remaining holes open, then close one or more of the others to get the required pitch. The downside to this technique is that the cross fingerings are not always identical on different instruments.

Let's use the fourth of the scale (*fa*) as an example again. Play the fifth (*so*) by closing just the thumbhole. Leaving the highest fingerhole open, close all the others and listen to the note produced. If the note seems a little flat, try opening the lowest fingerhole. One of these fingerings should give you the fourth of the scale and opening one more fingerhole should give you the sharp fourth or flat fifth of the scale. Again, a chromatic tuner is useful for checking the intonation of the various cross fingerings.

Here are examples of chromatic scales using cross fingering, although you may need to adapt these a little for your own instrument - if a cross fingered note is sharp, close an extra fingerhole; if it is flat try opening another one. Also, notice that the low sharp fifth/flat sixth of the scale is played by half holing as there is no cross fingering option for this note.

Here is a cross fingered chromatic scale on a C instrument:

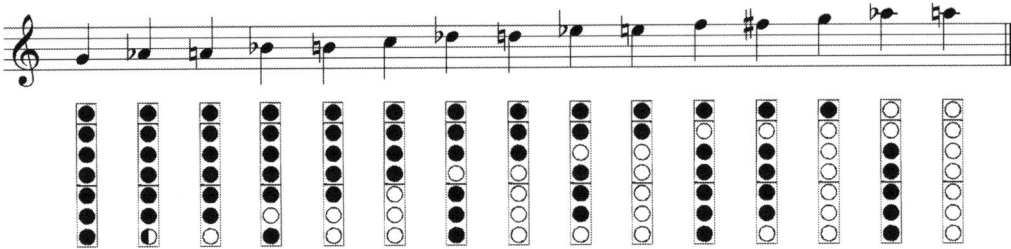

Here is a cross fingered chromatic scale on a G instrument:

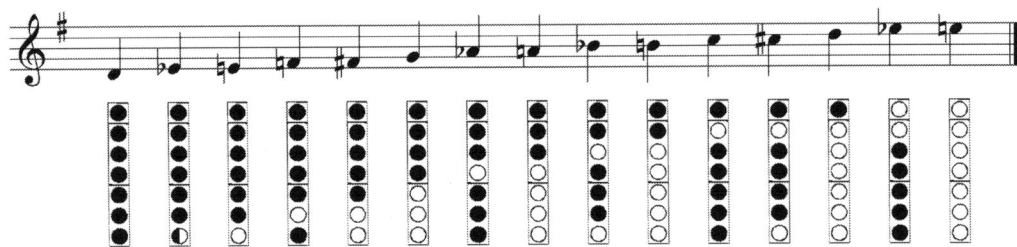

PLAYING IN OTHER KEYS

As mentioned earlier, the bawu and hulusi are like the harmonica in that they are available in a wide range of different keys. Also like the harmonica, it is possible to play them in additional keys besides the one stamped on them. Before getting into the reasons why you might want to do that, let's sidetrack a little with some discussion of scales.

A lot of traditional music from all over the world uses pentatonic scales. As the name suggests, these are scales that have five notes per octave, unlike the seven notes of the familiar diatonic major scale (*do re mi fa so la ti*), or the twelve notes of the Western chromatic scale. There are various different types of pentatonic scales, but the two most common are called the major pentatonic and the minor pentatonic.

The major pentatonic uses the first, second, third, fifth and sixth notes of the major scale - *do re mi so la*. Here is the major pentatonic starting on the keynote (*do*) for C and G instruments:

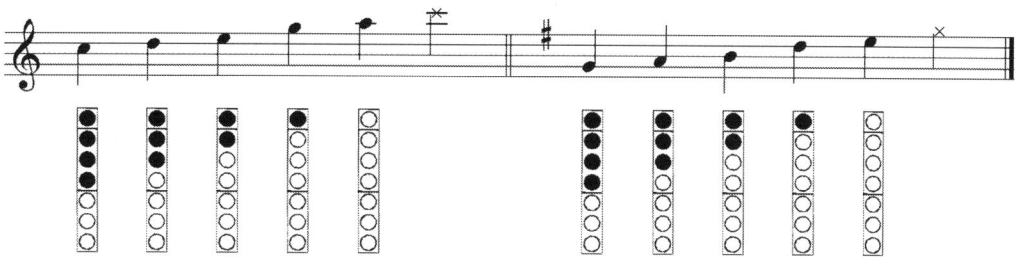

One thing should strike you straight away - that there is no octave repeat of the keynote, or high *do*. This is no problem for many tunes - for example, "Amazing Grace" is a well known pentatonic tune that doesn't require that high *do* note, but does need some pitches in the lower octave; many traditional tunes for the bawu and hulusi are similarly structured. However, there are quite a few tunes that do require the high *do* and possibly some other upper octave notes too. The solution to this is treat another note as the keynote.

The most common alternative key uses the lowest normal note as the keynote. On a C instrument, this would put you in the key of G; on a G instrument, this would put you in the key of D. Here is the major pentatonic scale again, this time with the lowest note of the instrument as the keynote:

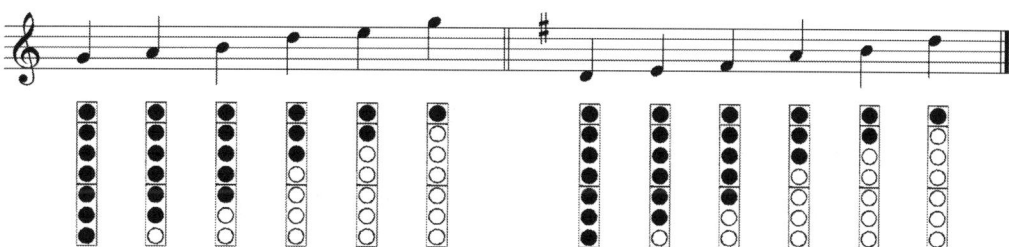

You can also play a complete major scale from keynote to octave this way (note that the seventh note of the scale (*ti*) can be played either by half holing or cross fingering:

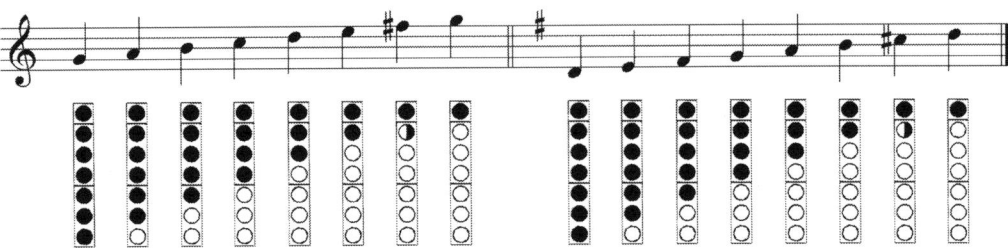

The minor pentatonic is very closely related to the major pentatonic scale. If you take the same notes as the major pentatonic, but play them against *la* rather than *do*, you get the relative minor pentatonic scale - *la do re mi so*. In Western music theory, A minor is the relative minor key to the key of C major - they both use the same key signature (no sharps or flats) and they are treated similarly in Chinese music. In fact, the usual drone notes of a twin drone hulusi in the key of C would be A and E (*LA* and *mi*) which helps outline the Am tonality.

A full octave of the minor pentatonic relative to the designated key of the instrument can be played like this:

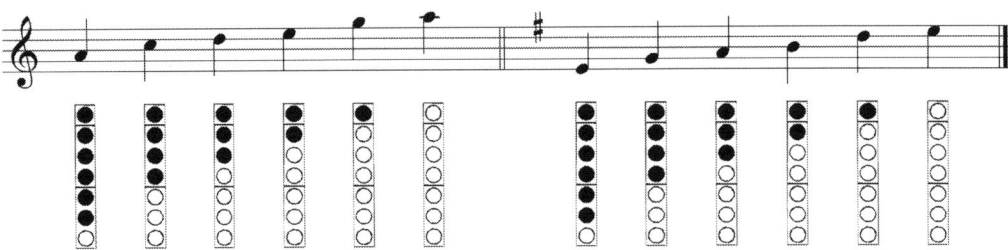

Tunes in the minor mode are as common in Chinese music as tunes in the major mode, with many tunes moving freely between the two.

The relative minor pentatonic to the above mentioned alternative key position can also be played across a full octave by starting on the underblown note:

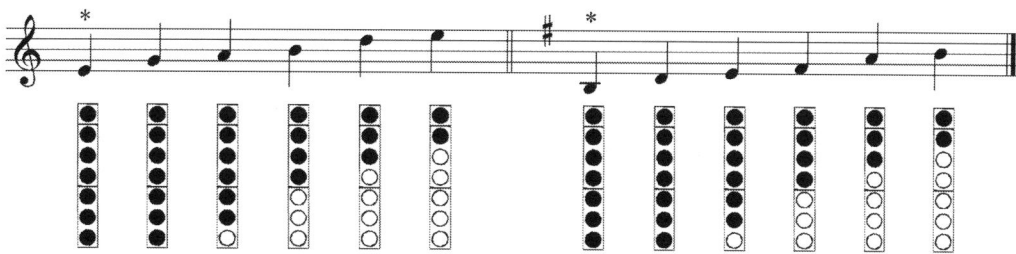

This also gives you a couple of notes in the upper octave that might be useful for some tunes. There are several other additional key positions used on the bawu and hulusi, but the aforementioned are by far the most common. The relative key positions are usually described in terms of how the lowest "normal" note (ie not the underblown one) functions in the scale. In the designated key of the instrument, the lowest note is the low fifth (*SO*) of the scale, so this is described as "all holes closed = 5". In the alternate key position described above, the lowest note is being treated as the keynote, so this is described as "all holes closed = 1".

If you have no musical background at all, some of this might seem a little confusing at first. Don't worry - in the next chapter we'll look at some practical examples to help you make sense of it all. In the meantime and for possible future reference, here are charts comparing the major scales in the four most common key positions, for both C and G instruments. As usual, you may need to adjust the cross fingerings to suit your instrument, or use half holing instead.

C instrument, all holes closed = 5

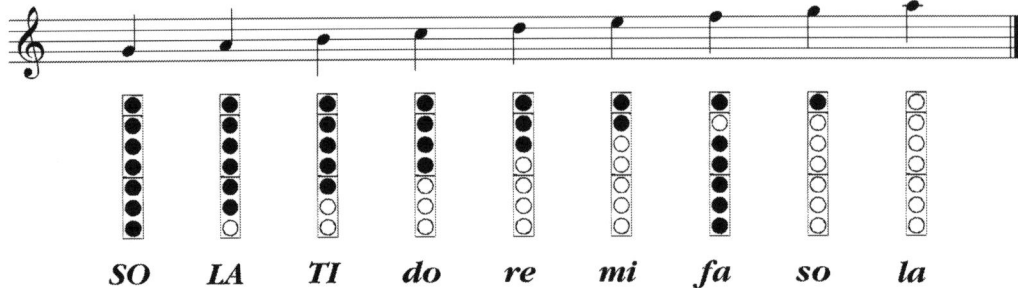

C instrument, all holes closed = 1

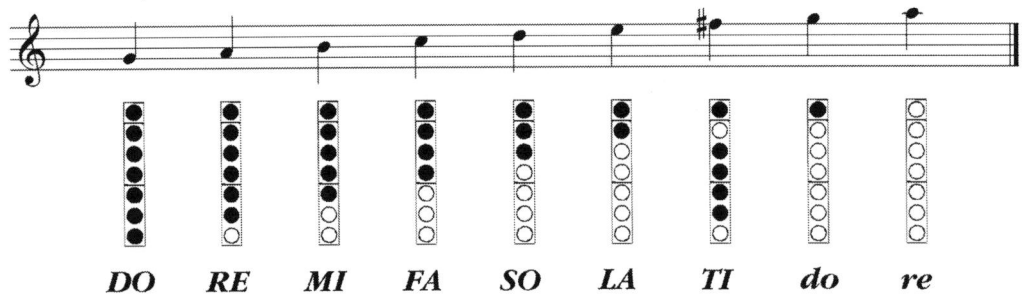

C instrument, all holes closed = 2

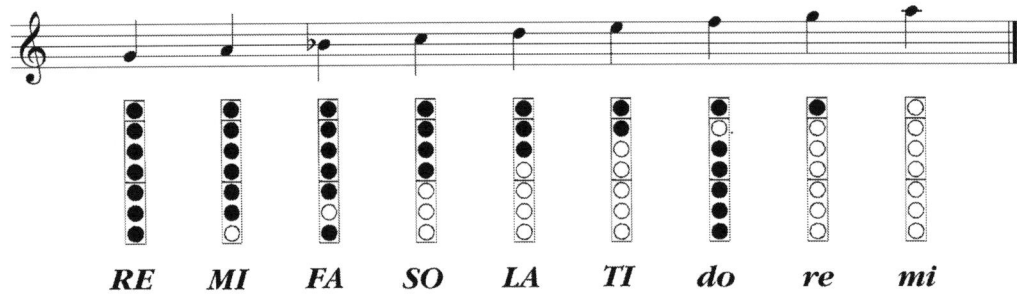

C instrument, all holes closed = 4

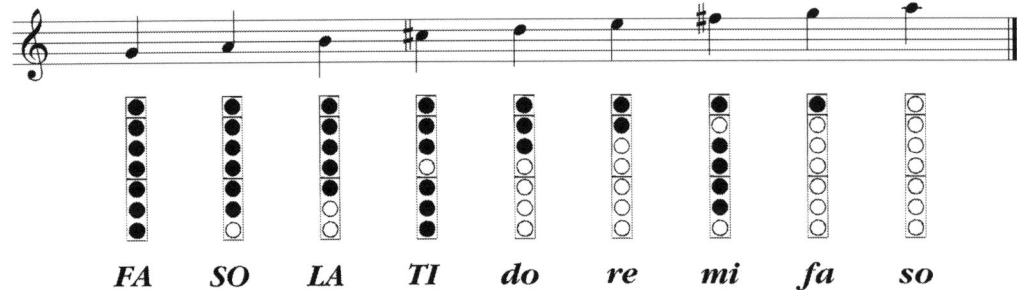

G instrument, all holes closed = 5

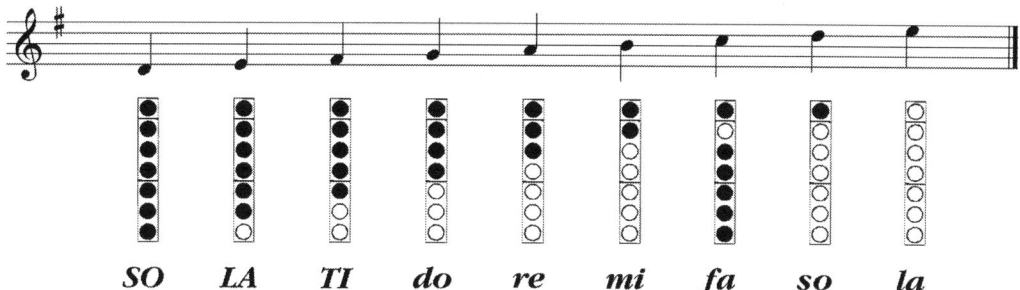

G instrument, all holes closed = 1

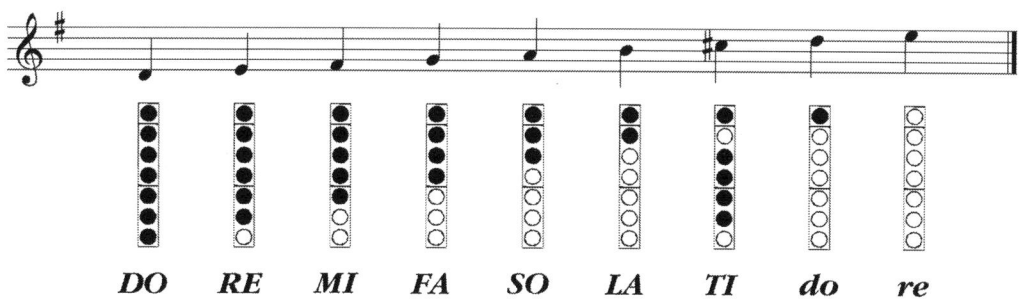

G instrument, all holes closed = 2

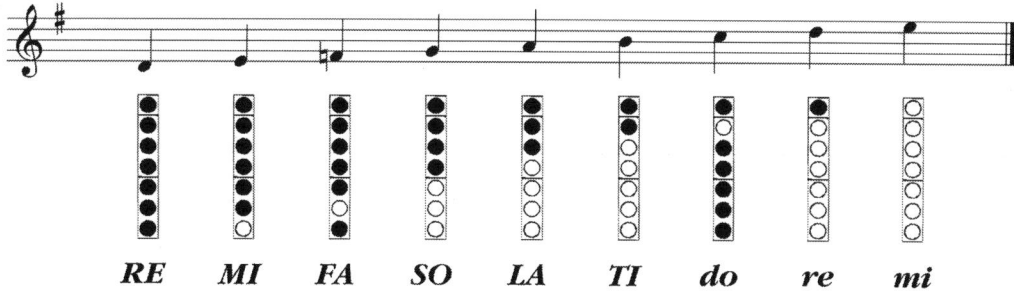

G instrument, all holes closed = 4

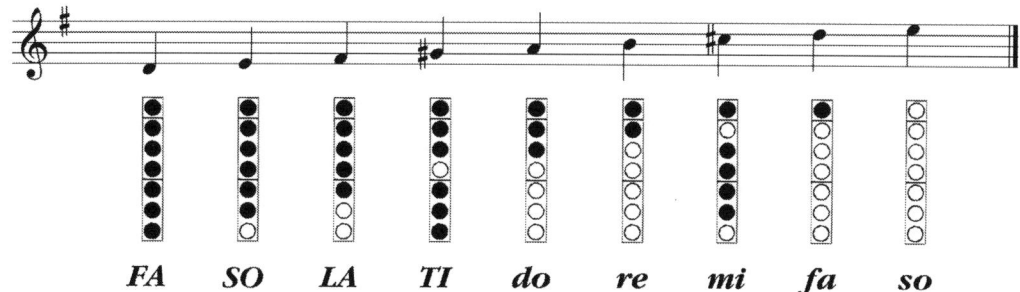

FAMILIAR WESTERN TUNES

In this chapter we will look at a few well-known Western melodies, presented in both standard notation and tablature, to help further familiarise you with your instrument.

AMAZING GRACE

This well known hymn was written in the late 18th century and the lyrics were later set to a tune called "New Britain", in which form it is most often heard today. It is an excellent example of a pentatonic tune that lies perfectly on the bawu or hulusi in its designated key.

AULD LANG SYNE

Traditionally sung at the start of the New Year, the words were written by the famous Scottish poet Robert Burns and set to the tune of an older folk song. It is almost, but not quite pentatonic, having the lower seventh (*TI*) added. The melody covers the full range of the bawu and hulusi, from the lowest normal note with all holes closed, to the highest note with all holes open.

LONDON BRIDGE

The tune of this familiar nursery rhyme includes the fourth note of the scale (*fa*), which is shown in the tab as a cross fingered note, but could also be played by half holing. Try practising it both ways to see what works best for you.

The same tune can also be played in the "all holes closed = 1" position. In fact, it is probably easier to play in this position, as it doesn't require the use cross fingering or half holing.

SCARBOROUGH FAIR

This British folksong is probably best known from the 1966 version by Simon and Garfunkel. The tune is in what Western musical terminology calls the Dorian mode, which is a minor scale with a natural sixth degree. This translates to the raised fourth degree of the bawu/hulusi's basic scale (*fi*), which is shown in the tab as a cross fingered note, but again it's a good idea to try it with the half holed version as well. If you have a hulusi, then you may want to switch on your drone pipe(s) for this tune!

EL CONDOR PASA

Another tune made famous by Simon and Garfunkel, "El Condor Pasa" was written in 1913 by the Peruvian composer Daniel Alomía Robles, based on traditional songs of the Andes. Actually, only the first part of the tune is playable on a traditional bawu or hulusi (although the second section is playable if you have an extended range instrument), but it does illustrate the use of the underblown note right at the start, as well as the sharp fifth of the scale (*SI*) played by half holing.

AMAZING GRACE

C instrument   Traditional

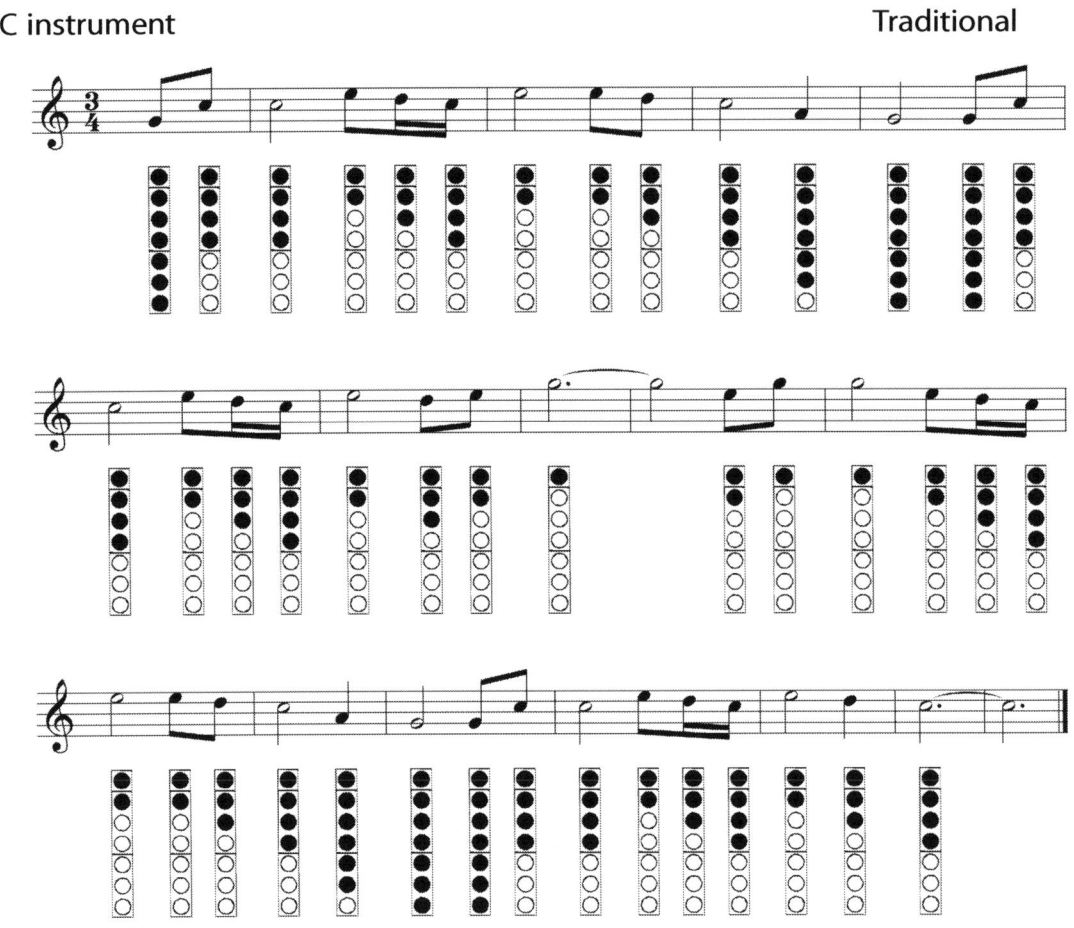

AMAZING GRACE

G instrument Traditional

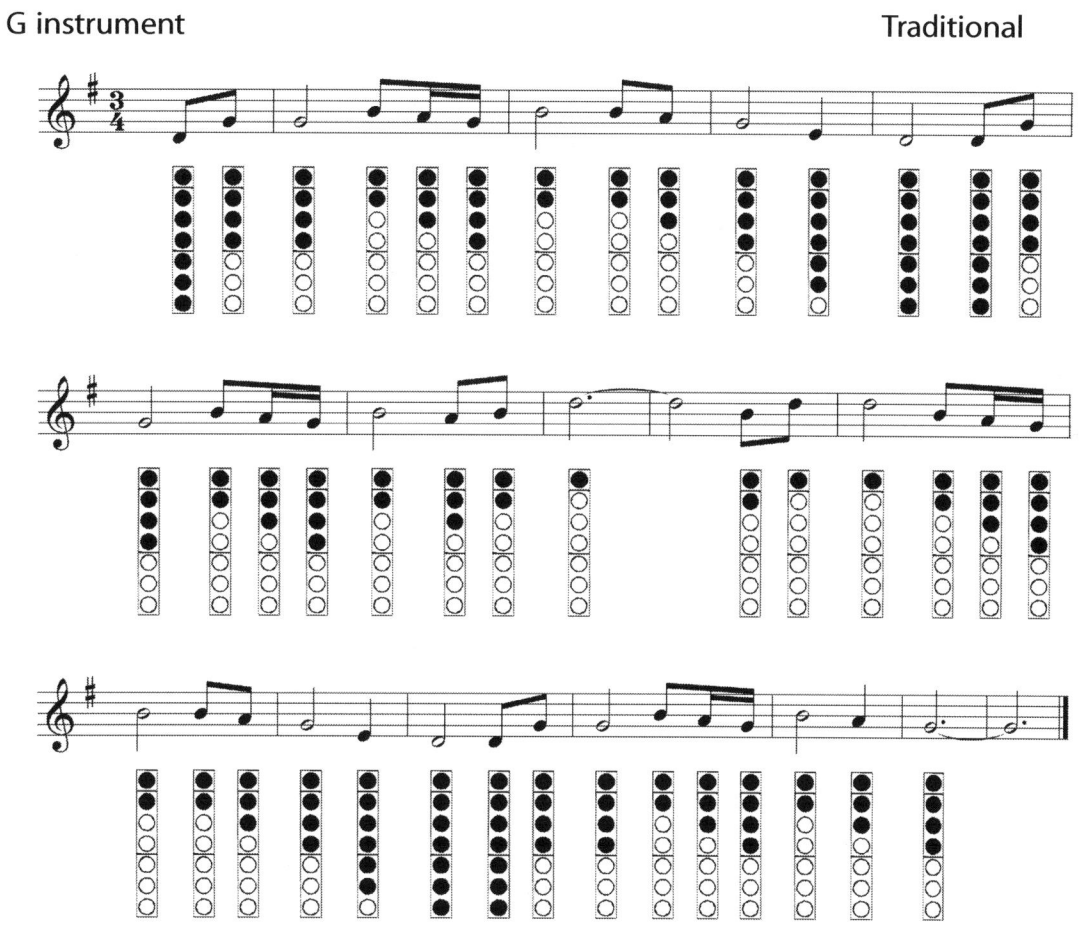

AULD LANG SYNE

C instrument Traditional

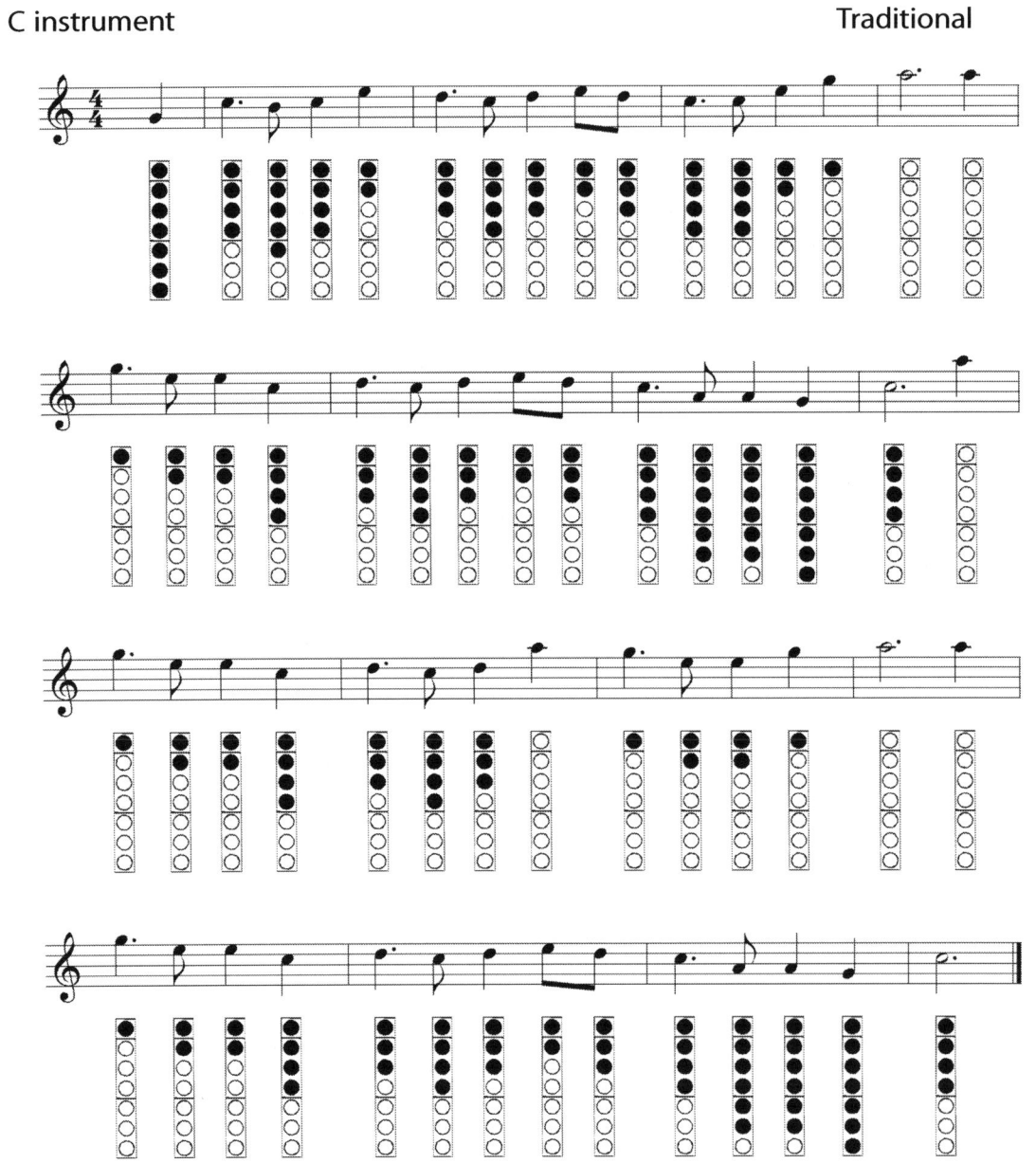

AULD LANG SYNE

G instrument Traditional

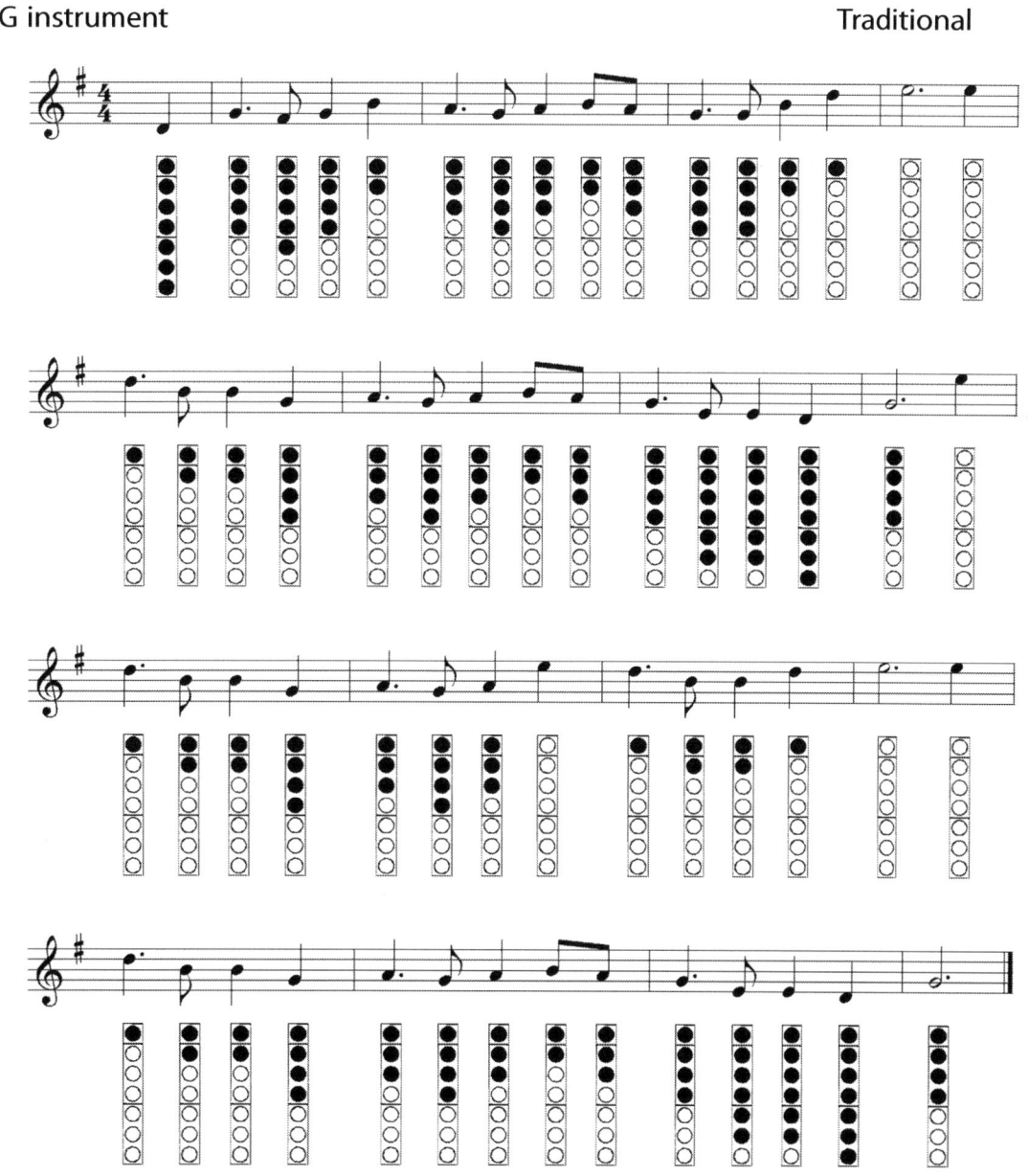

LONDON BRIDGE

C, all holes closed = 5   Traditional

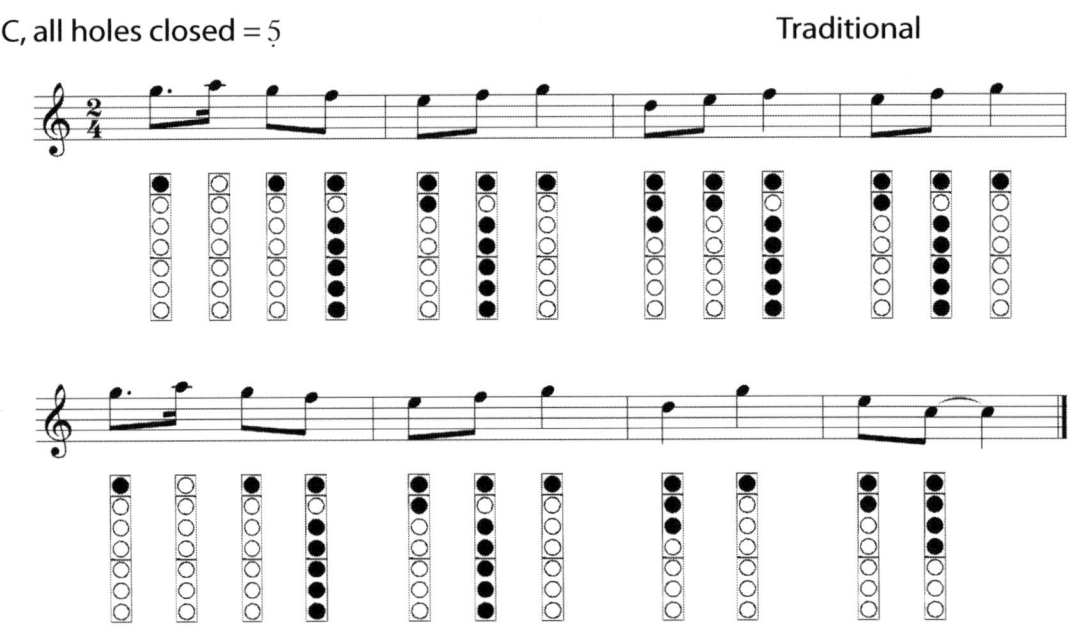

LONDON BRIDGE

C, all holes closed = 1   Traditional

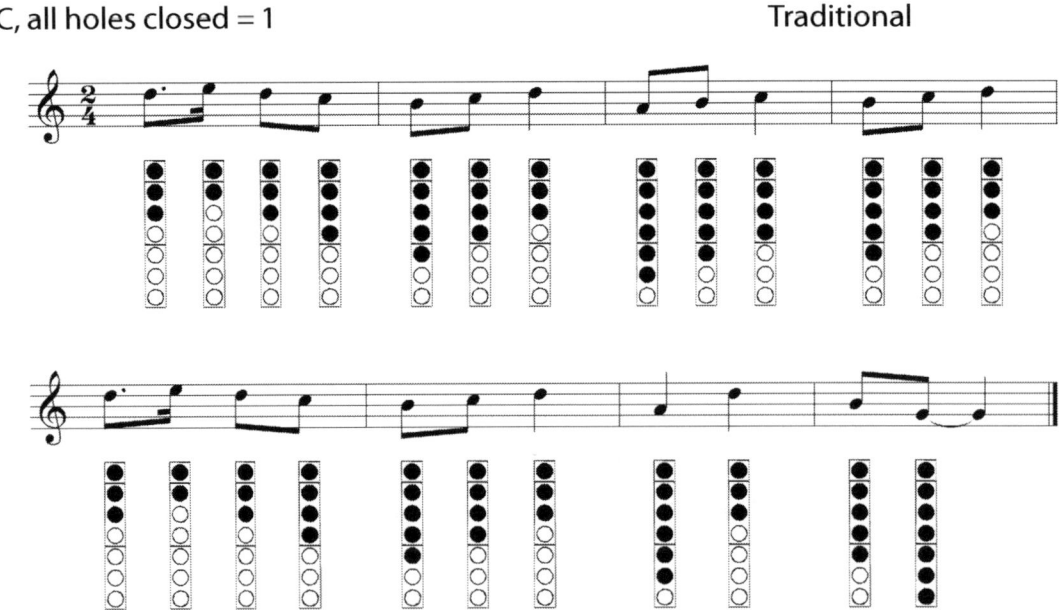

LONDON BRIDGE

G, all holes closed = 5

Traditional

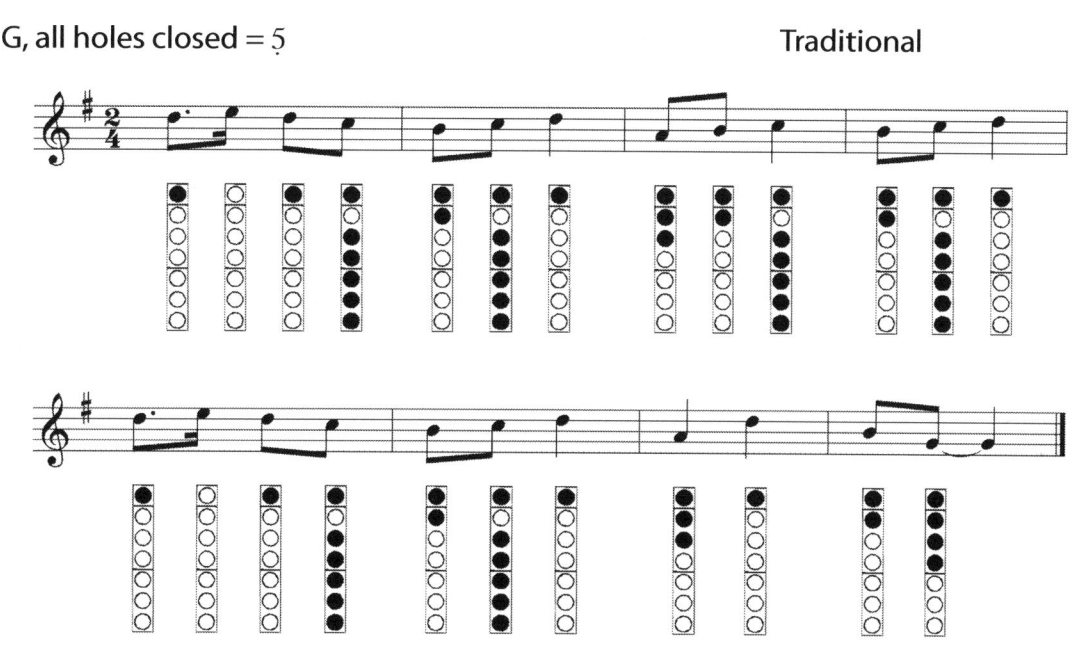

LONDON BRIDGE

G, all holes closed = 1

Traditional

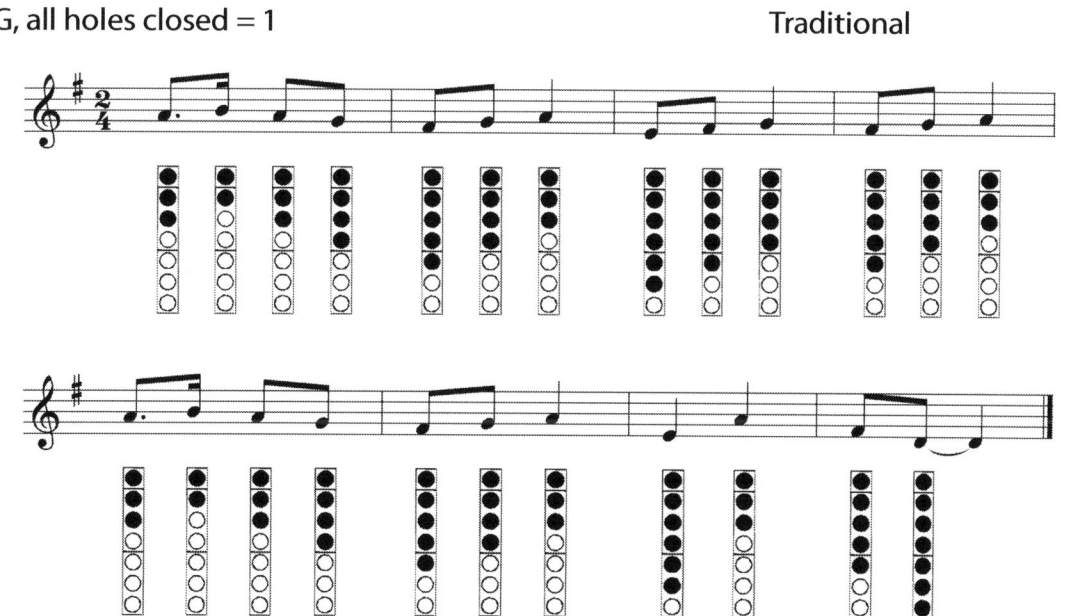

SCARBOROUGH FAIR

C instrument Traditional

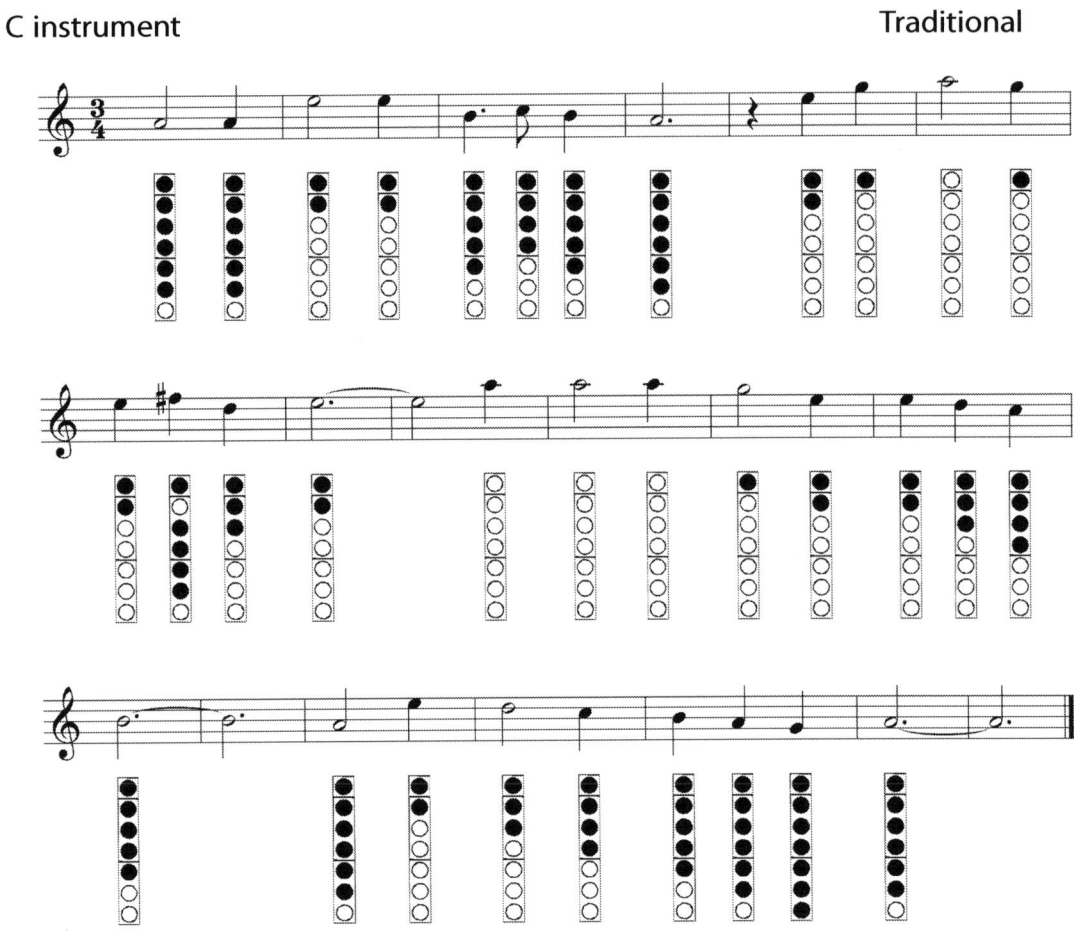

48

SCARBOROUGH FAIR

G instrument Traditional

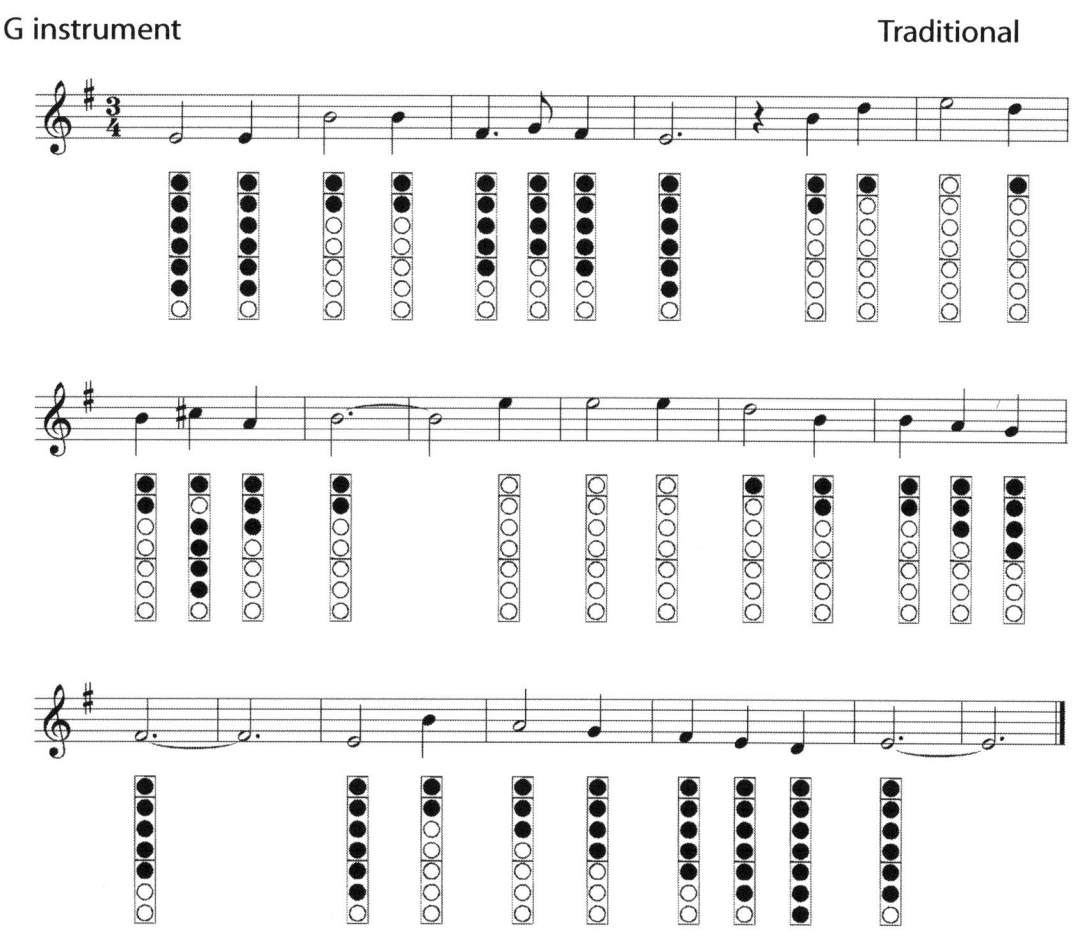

EL CONDOR PASA

C instrument
Daniel Alomía Robles

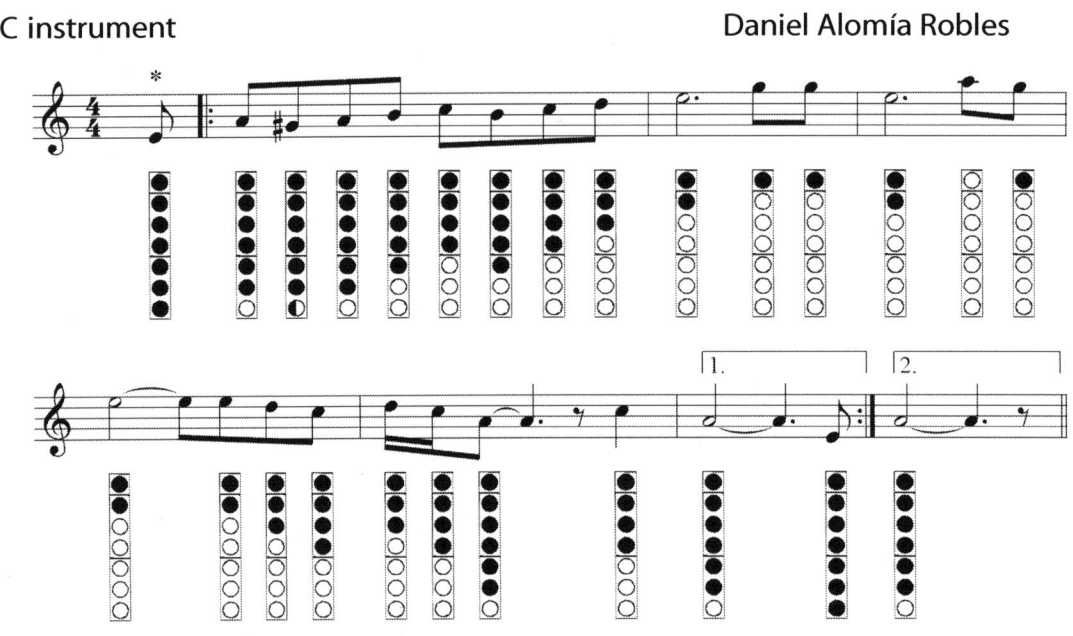

EL CONDOR PASA

G instrument
Daniel Alomía Robles

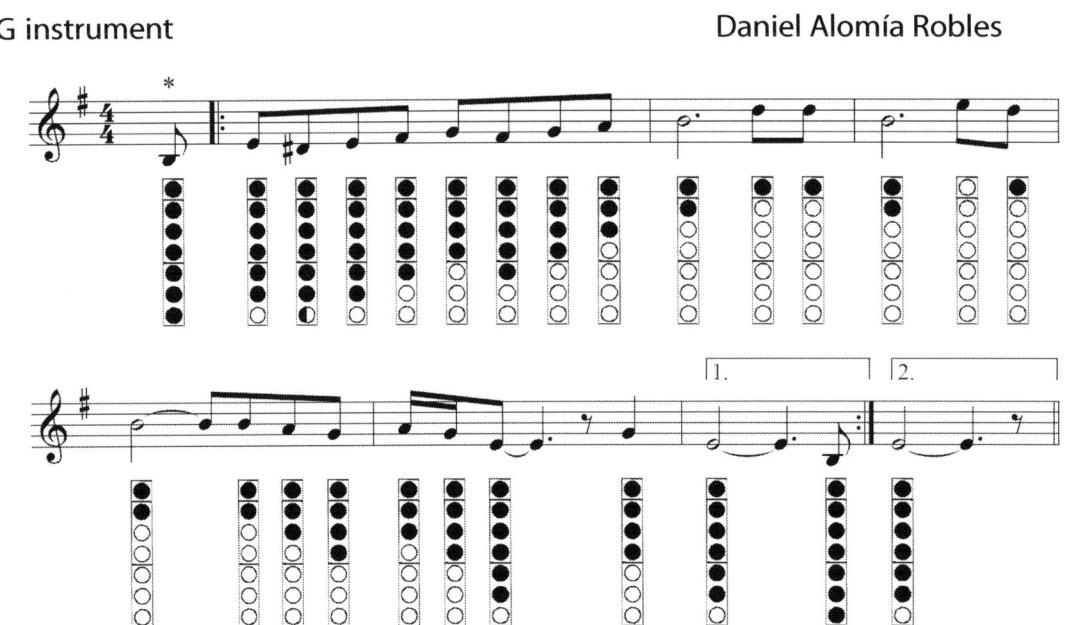

TRADITIONAL CHINESE TUNES

By now, you should be quite familiar with the layout of your instrument, so it's time to move on to some traditional Chinese tunes without the use of tablature as "training wheels". There are a dozen tunes in this chapter, ranging from quite easy to moderately challenging. Most of them are played in the "all holes closed = $\underset{.}{5}$" position, but I have included a few examples of some other key positions. Certain aspects of some of the tunes may perhaps sound a little unfamiliar to Western ears - for example, some pieces end on notes other than the key note, others use phrases with an unusual number of bars, etc. To help give you an idea of how they should sound, audio examples of each tune are available for free download from my website. I would also strongly encourage you to seek out recordings by professional players of the bawu and hulusi, to get a feel for the traditional performance styles, as there are many aspects of music that cannot be easily represented on the printed page. Another thing to keep in mind, is that there is no single definitive version of a folk tune. Traditional players will rarely play a tune exactly the same way twice, so feel free to vary your performances as you see fit. Just treat the songs with respect and you can't go too far wrong.

GOLDEN PEACOCK JUMPS LIGHTLY

To the Dai the peacock is a symbol of good luck, happiness and prosperity, so it is not surprising that this bird features in the names of so many of their folk songs and dances. Although it is quite a simple tune, there are a lot of grace notes in this piece, along with some use of portamento - it may be easier to learn the basic tune first and add in these embellishments later.

SONG OF YIMENG MOUNTAIN

This famous folk song from Shandong Province has had quite a few different rhythmic settings. The version presented here is in simple waltz time, like the recent hit version by popular Chinese singer Zhang Yan. Look out for the underblown note in the next to last bar.

LADY MENG JIANG

Meng Jiang was a legendary Chinese figure whose husband was sent to work on the building of the Great Wall of China. Upon learning of his death, her tears caused a section of the Great Wall to collapse, revealing the bones of her husband and countless other workers buried there. This tune is a favorite of erhu players, but its range also fits the bawu and hulusi perfectly.

LOVE SONG OF KANG DING

This beautiful folk melody from Sichuan Province was originally titled "Horse Riding High Upon The Mountain Side". It was rearranged, retitled and had lyrics written to it in the 1940s by Wu Wen Ji and it recently inspired a movie with the same title. This tune works particularly well with the drones of the hulusi.

EMBROIDERING THE POUCH

There are quite a few different tunes with this title, which refers to the custom of embroidering a small purse or pouch for a gift for a loved one, especially one who has to travel far from home. This particular version is from Yunnan Province and has long been a favorite of bawu and hulusi players.

MIAO MINORITY SONG

The Hmong people have communities all over Asia, as well as in the US and other parts of the world. In China, where they are one of the 56 officially recognised minority groups, they are known by the Chinese name Miao. They traditionally play a bawu-like instrument called tsaaj nplaim (sometimes spelled dja mblai and often simply called Hmong flute) and in recent years the hulusi has become quite popular with them. This traditional Hmong tune is played in the "all holes = 1" position.

WHEN THE MOON RISES

A beautiful melody from the Wa or Va people, who are found both in Northern Myanmar (formally Burma) and over the border in Yunnan Province, China. They play versions of the hulusi known as beiban and baihongliao in their language. Pay attention to the eighth bar, which consists of the lowest normal note immediately followed by the underblown note - these both use the same fingering, the notes being selected by breath pressure. The same notes occur at the start of the following bar, but this time in the reverse order. Try to get the change from normal to underblown and vice versa as smooth as you can.

THE TERRACES

This tune is from the Hani minority, who have a legend about the origin of the bawu. Once upon a time, a young Hani boy and girl fell in love, but a demon wanted the girl for himself. He tried to force her to swear a wedding vow to him, but she refused to speak, so the demon cut out her tongue in a fit of rage and abandoned her in a forest. A bird found the girl's tongue and told her to place it into a length of bamboo and use it to call for her lover. The young man heard her plaintive music and came to rescue her and kill the demon. The young man's was Ba and his sweetheart's name was Wu - this is how the bawu got its name and since then, it has traditionally been used for lovers to express their feelings for one another.

The title of this tune refers to the spectacular terraced rice fields of the Hani people in Yuanyang County, Yunnan Province, covering many thousands of acres and dating back more than 1300 years. This tune is usually played with some fairly crisp articulation, so I've added some tonguing suggestions, but feel free to play it the way you think it sounds best.

LUSHENG DANCE

The lusheng is a kind of mouth organ played by various minority groups in China, in particular the Hmong or Miao People, to whom it serves as a symbol of cultural identity. Playing of the lusheng is often combined with challenging dance movements and lusheng festivals are regularly held, featuring massed performances and contests to find the best players.

This tune could be played with a staccato feel to it using double tonguing, or alternatively you could use a less percussive attack to the notes. Try it each way and see what sounds best to you.

LUQUAN FOLK SONG

A folk song from Luquan Yi and Miao Autonomous County in Yunnan Province. This arrangement is in the "all holes = 4" position and requires cross fingering and/or half holing to play the chromatic notes. Pay attention also to the middle section of the tune which has phrases of five bars in length, in contrast to the four bar phrases of the first and last sections.

THE LITTLE FLOWING STREAM

Also translated with various similar titles such as "The Rippling Brook", this is beautiful melody originating from Midu County in the Dali Bai Autonomous Prefecture of southern Yunnan Province. This arrangement is played in the "all holes = 2" position and you will need either cross fingering or half holing to play the fourth note of the designated scale (which functions as the key note of the major scale in the "all holes = 2" position): pick whichever technique allows you to play the melody as flowingly as possible. Although the song is in 4/4 time, there are a couple of bars in 3/4 time, so look out for those. You can add vibrato to the long sustained notes, or you could simply play them as straight tones - your choice

MIDU FOLK SONG

Midu County in Yunnan Province is famous for the many folk songs that the area has contributed to the musical heritage of China. This one is simply called "Midu Folk Song", or "Midu Mountain Song" and is a firm favorite of singers and hulusi players.

GOLDEN PEACOCK JUMPS LIGHTLY

C instrument   Dai Folk Song

GOLDEN PEACOCK JUMPS LIGHTLY

G instrument   Dai Folk Song

SONG OF YIMENG MOUNTAIN

C instrument   Shandong Folk Song

SONG OF YIMENG MOUNTAIN

G instrument   Shandong Folk Song

LADY MENG JIANG

C instrument   Jiangsu Folk Song

LADY MENG JIANG

G instrument   Jiangsu Folk Song

LOVE SONG OF KANG DING

C instrument   Sichuan Folk Song

LOVE SONG OF KANG DING

G instrument   Sichuan Folk Song

EMBROIDERING THE POUCH

C instrument

Yunnan Folk Song

EMBROIDERING THE POUCH

G instrument

Yunnan Folk Song

MIAO MINORITY SONG

C instrument   Hmong Folk Song

MIAO MINORITY SONG

G instrument   Hmong Folk Song

WHEN THE MOON RISES

C instrument   Wa Folk Song

WHEN THE MOON RISES

G instrument   Wa Folk Song

THE TERRACES

C instrument Hani Folk Song

THE TERRACES

G instrument

Hani Folk Song

LUSHENG DANCE

C instrument

Hmong Folk Song

LUSHENG DANCE

G instrument

Hmong Folk Song

LUQUAN FOLK SONG

C instrument   Yunnan Folk Song

LUQUAN FOLK SONG

G instrument   Yunnan Folk Song

THE LITTLE FLOWING STREAM

C instrument   Yunnan Folk Song

THE LITTLE FLOWING STREAM

G instrument   Yunnan Folk Song

MIDU FOLK SONG

C instrument   Yunnan Folk Song

MIDU FOLK SONG

G instrument   Yunnan Folk Song

CARE AND MAINTENANCE

GENERAL CARE

As with most things, your bawu or hulusi will last longer if you take care of it. Don't drop it, don't sit on it and don't hit anyone with it. Avoid extremes of temperature, sudden changes in temperature and/or humidity and don't leave it in direct sunlight. A protective case is a worthwhile investment, but be sure to let your instrument dry out thoroughly after playing before storing it in a case. Hulusi and upright bawu are best left to dry with the mouthpiece pointing downwards, to let any residual moisture drain away from the reed. Traditional bawu are probably best left to air out with the mouthpiece pointing upwards. Avoid placing it near a heater to try to speed up the drying process - a sudden change in humidity can cause gourd and bamboo to crack.

If you do develop any cracks in your instrument, these can be filled with a cyanoacrylate adhesive (SuperGlue, Crazy Glue, etc.), the gel types being best suited for larger cracks. Apply a small amount to the crack, let it set for a while, then trim off any excess with a scalpel or craft knife.

If you notice any fine sawdust-like material falling from the instrument as you play, immediately stop playing and start looking for small holes in the instrument, about the size of pin pricks. These are the telltale signs of woodworm and if you spot them, my advice would be to get the affected instrument out of your house as soon as possible. Plan A for such an infestation would be to burn the instrument. You may be reluctant to do this if you invested substantial effort or financial outlay into obtaining your instrument and if so, there is a Plan B. Let it dry out for a while (preferably outdoors, to avoid any risk of spreading the bugs to any other wood in your home), then wrap it in plastic as airtightly as possible and place it in a freezer. After a few weeks, take it out and let it sit at normal temperature for a while, then recheck for fresh sawdust. If all is well, get back to playing and hope you caught it before it spread to anything else. If you start to notice the sawdust again and any fresh holes, go to Plan A.

REED CARE AND ADJUSTMENT

Rinsing out your mouth before playing is always a good idea, as any stray particles of food can get lodged in the reed and stop it from working properly. It's also probably wise not to share your bawu or hulusi with anyone else. If the instrument suddenly stops making any sound, the most likely cause is a stuck reed. With the traditional bawu, the reed is easy to access, but with the hulusi or upright bawu you will need to disassemble the instrument to get at the reed. With more modern instruments, the pipes can usually be quite easily pulled from the windchest, but in older or more cheaply made ones, the pipes may be glued in place. If this is the case, then you may be able to pick the glue from the joint and pull out the pipe, then reglue it after you are done. Once you have access to the reed, take a close look at it before doing anything else.

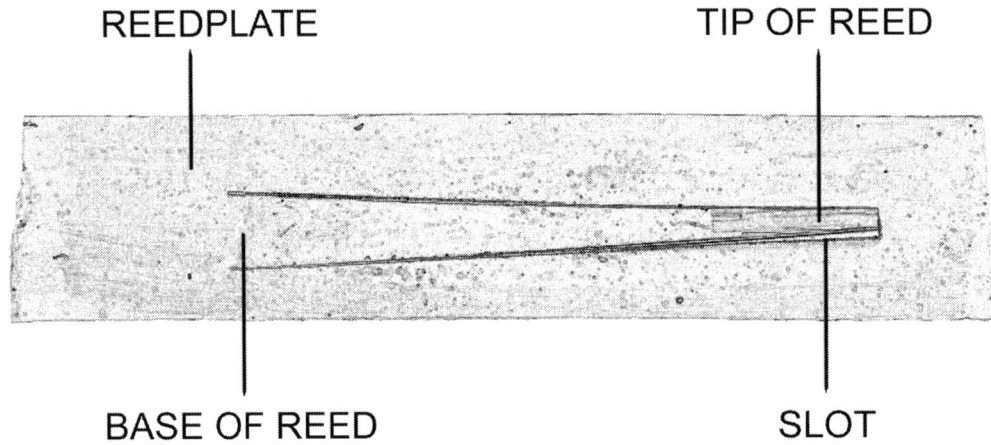

WARNING - REEDS ARE VERY DELICATE THINGS!
Be extremely careful when working on them.

The reed consists of a small triangle cut from a thin brass plate, with the base of the triangle left attached and the rest of the reed sitting above a triangular slot through which it should be able to swing back and forth without obstruction. The free end of the reed should sit slightly higher than the rest of the reed and the surrounding brass. If the reed appears to be stuck, try gently tracing around the edges of the reed with a fine needle and see if you can free it. An alcohol soaked cotton swab may also help remove any sticky deposits that may be interfering with the working of the reed, but be sure to swab from the base of the reed towards the tip, to reduce the chances of snagging the reed. If you gently pluck the tip of the reed you should hear a "twang" that has a definite pitch. If the reed has a nice amount of springiness, but makes an unclear sound when plucked, there might some deposits along the edges of the reed or slot preventing the reed from vibrating freely. However, if the reed is lacking in springiness and the tip of the reed tends to settle below the level of the surrounding brass, then it's probable that the reed has succumbed to metal fatigue - you may even be able to see a small crack at the base of the reed. If this is the case, then your only option is to see if your supplier can send you a replacement reed, or replace the whole instrument.

Sometimes the reed can benefit from a slight adjustment. At the risk of repeating myself:

WARNING - REEDS ARE VERY DELICATE THINGS!

Messing with the reed will probably invalidate any guarantee or warranty, plus you run the risk of making your instrument unplayable. If you have the slightest doubt in your ability to adjust a reed carefully, it's best to leave things well alone and learn to put up with any inconsistencies in your instrument's playability. Also, it's important to wait until you're reasonably well practised at playing before deciding that your instrument requires a adjustment - many things that seem like a fault with the instrument are more than likely due to a beginner's underdeveloped playing technique. That said, bawu and hulusi sometimes seem to respond better at one extreme of the range than at the other. If you find your instrument responds very well in the lower register, but the highest notes seem weak, then the tip of the reed may need to be raised a little. Carefully slide something thin and flexible under the reed and very gently lift it very slightly. Reassemble your instrument and play the scale from low to high. If the high notes are still less responsive than the lower ones, try lifting the reed a little more. Conversely, if the higher notes respond fine, but the lower register has a rather harsh buzzing tone to it, that is a sign that the reed may be set too high. To remedy this, push gently downwards near the base of the reed using a matchstick or toothpick.

To summarise - to improve the response in the higher register, set the tip of the reed higher; to improve the response in the lower register, set the tip of the reed lower.

The reed of a traditional bawu is somewhat exposed, so it's not a bad idea to make a cover to keep it safe. This is easily done by taking a strip of thin card about 1" wide by 3" long, wrapping it around the bawu at the mouthpiece and taping the free end to the rest of the card, forming a cover that can be slid away from the mouthpiece when you want to play, then slid back over it when not in use.

TUNING

Unlike a guitar or violin, you won't have to tune your bawu or hulusi every time you want to play it, but most bawu and some, but not all hulusi, have a joint that allows the overall pitch level to be adjusted. With upright bawu, the joint is usually inside the windchest. Sliding the instrument apart at this joint lowers the pitch; pushing it together raises the pitch. This is useful if you wish to play with other musicians, or to play along with a recording that doesn't quite match the pitch of your instrument. Some occasional lubrication of this joint is not a bad idea - a small amount of lip balm works well, as does a dab of vaseline.

It is also possible to adjust the pitch of individual notes if they do not seem quite in tune. Notes can be lowered by partly closing the highest fingerhole that's left open when you finger the note you wish to tune. This can be done in a temporary manner using a small piece of tape at the edge of the fingerhole. Notes can be raised in pitch by slightly widening the highest fingerhole left often - as this requires filing away some of the material, this is a little less temporary. If you change your mind after increasing the size of the hole, you can use tape to close up the hole a little, but this is obviously a situation where the old adage "measure twice, cut once" is particularly appropriate.

NONSTANDARD INSTRUMENTS

The instruments described so far in this book will correspond with 95% of the bawu and hulusi you are likely to encounter, but for the sake of completeness, there are a few less common versions that may be worth brief mention.

DOUBLE INSTRUMENTS

Both double bawu and double hulusi are available that combine two instruments into one. In the case of the bawu and upright bawu, they are literally two normal bawu in different keys joined together, so that the mouthpieces are in closer proximity to each other. This allows the player to change keys quickly in the middle of a piece, or to play a tune that requires a wider range than is available on a normal bawu. The most common key combinations are G/C and F/Bb.

Double hulusi usually have a single windchest, but have a pair of melody pipes. Sometimes each pipe has its own mouthpiece, or in some cases the instrument has a single mouthpiece and the player has to make a small mechanical adjustment to the pipe to enable it to sound. As with double bawu, the key combinations of G/C and F/Bb are most common, but you can also find such combinations as C/Bb, low F/high F, etc.

Not surprisingly, there are also triple bawu and hulusi, with three instruments combined into one.

UNUSUAL DRONE NOTES

The drone note of a single drone hulusi is usually tuned to the third note (*mi*) of the designated key, ie the same pitch as you get with the thumbhole and highest fingerhole closed. If a second drone is present, it is usually tuned to the low sixth (*LA*), the note produced with just the lowest fingerhole open. These drones are most effective with minor flavoured tunes - those that tend to end on *LA*.

However, I have one older hulusi in the key of G with a single drone note tuned to D, the same as the lowest normal note of the instrument (*SO*). I have seen transcriptions of field recordings from Yunnan that show instruments with a similar drone, as well as some with a high fifth (*so*) drone. These drones would work well with major key tunes in both the "all holes closed = 5" position and the "all holes closed = 1" position.

KEYS AND DOUBLE FINGERHOLES

I've briefly touched on this topic in the chapter on additional playing techniques. Some recently made bawu and hulusi have double fingerholes to make half holed notes much more accurate and easy to play. Some others have finger keys similar to those used on standard Western woodwind instruments. Most often, these add the fourth note of the basic scale (*fa*), or extend the upper and/or lower ranges. Usually the rest of the scale is fingered normally, but if your instrument did not come with a chart to demonstrate the additional pitches, you may want to contact your dealer to see if they can supply one.

ADDITIONAL FINGERHOLES

Standard bawu and hulusi have seven holes - six fingerholes and one thumbhole. Recently some instruments have been produced that have eight or nine holes.

With the eight hole bawu or hulusi, the thumb closes the hole at the rear, the first three fingers of the left hand cover the three highest fingerholes and the remaining holes are closed with the four fingers of the right hand. Eight holed bawu and hulusi produce the same notes with all holes closed as a standard instrument - *MI* as an underblown tone and *SO* as the lowest normal note. Opening each hole in turn produces the scale *LA, TI, do, re, mi, so, la* and finally high *do* with all holes open.

Here are the notes produced by an eight hole bawu or hulusi in the key of C:

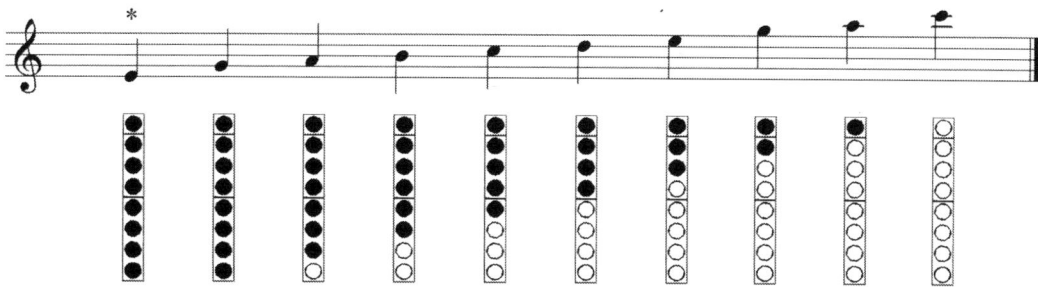

With the nine hole bawu or hulusi, the thumb closes the hole at the rear, the four fingers of the left hand cover the four highest fingerholes and the remaining holes are closed with the four fingers of the right hand. Nine holed bawu and hulusi produce the same notes with all holes closed as a standard instrument - *MI* as an underblown tone and *SO* as the lowest normal note. Opening each hole in turn produces the scale *LA, TI, do, re, mi, so, la*, high *do* and finally high *re* with all holes open.

Here are the notes produced by a nine hole instrument in the key of C:

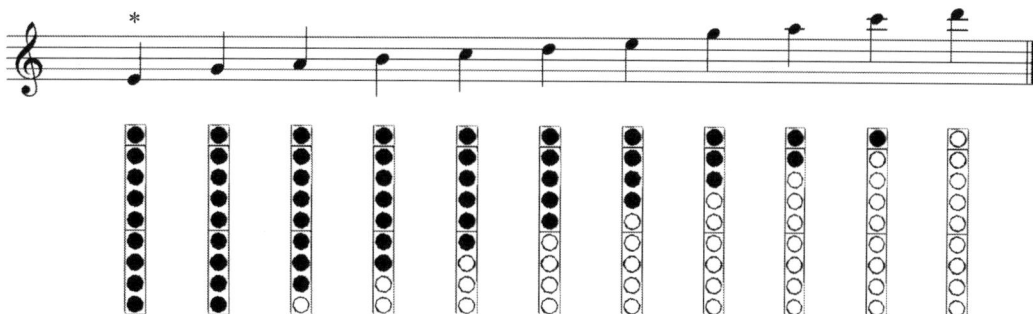

READING JIANPU NOTATION

Jianpu is the name of the numbered musical notation widely used in China and other parts of Asia. If you search on the Internet for bawu and hulusi tunes in Western notation, you are not likely to have much success. However, there is no shortage of tunes in jianpu notation and the basics of jianpu are quite straightforward to learn.

PITCH

The notes of the major scale are represented by the numbers 1 2 3 4 5 6 7, in the same way that solfege uses *do re mi fa so la ti*. At the start of a piece of jianpu notation will be something like "1=C", to indicate that the keynote of the scale is C and that 1 2 3 4 5 6 7 corresponds with C D E F G A B. If the notation indicates "1=G", then 1 2 3 4 5 6 7 will correspond with G A B C D E F#, etc.

Octaves are indicated by dots above or below a number. A number with a dot above it is on octave higher than a number without a dot. A dot below a number indicates that it is an octave lower. Two dots equals two octaves and so on.

Sharps and flats are indicated by the same symbols as used in Western notation (♯ and ♭) placed before a number.

TIMING

Time signatures are notated similarly to Western music, written as a fraction with the upper number showing how many beats there are to a bar and the lower number showing what note value constitutes one beat.

A number by itself represents a quarter note. A line under the number shortens it to an eighth note, two lines shortens it to a sixteenth note, etc. The underlines may be joined together under a group of notes. Dashes after a note lengthen it, each dash equal to the length of a quarter note. A dot after the note increases its length by half and two dots increases by three-quarters, similar to Western notation.

RESTS

0 is used to represent a rest, a duration of time where there is no note sounded. A plain 0 indicates a quarter note rest, an underlined 0 an eighth note rest, a double underlined 0 a sixteenth note rest, etc. For rests of longer than a quarter note, the 0 is repeated. For example, a full bar rest in 4/4 time would be written as | 0 0 0 0 |

OTHER SYMBOLS

Bar lines are similar to Western notion - a vertical line to mark the end of a measure, two vertical lines to represent a double bar line and a pair of vertical lines, one thin and one thick, to represent the end bar line. Repeat signs are usually the same as in Western notation (||: and :||). Ties, slurs and expression symbols are also similar to Western versions, except that they are always placed above the numbers. Staccato is often represented by small inverted triangles above the notes, as the dots used in Western notation could be confused with octave dots.

An additional piece of information is usually added for bawu and hulusi music, which indicates the note of the scale the lowest normal note of the instrument plays. For example:

全按作 $\underline{5}$

This is sometimes written as:

筒音作 $\underline{5}$

These are both equivalent to "all holes closed = $\underline{5}$", indicating that the lowest "normal" (ie not underblown) note is functioning as the low fifth of the scale for this tune - in other words, the keynote of the piece is the designated keynote of the instrument. The same set of characters followed by a 1 would indicate that the lowest normal note is functioning as the keynote of the piece and so on.

As an example, here is "Amazing Grace" again, this time written in jianpu:

AMAZING GRACE

All holes closed = 5̣   Traditional

$$\begin{array}{l} \tfrac{3}{4}\ \underline{5\dot{1}}|1 - \underline{3\,\underline{21}}|3 - \underline{3\,2}|1 - \underline{\dot{6}}|\dot{5} - \underline{\dot{5}\,1}| \\ 1 - \underline{3\,\underline{21}}|3 - \underline{2\,3}|5 - -|5 - \underline{3\,5}| \\ 5 - \underline{3\,\underline{21}}|3 - \underline{3\,2}|1 - \underline{\dot{6}}|\dot{5} - \underline{\dot{5}\,1}| \\ 1 - \underline{3\,\underline{21}}|3 - 2\ |1 - -|1 - -\ \| \end{array}$$

FINGERING CHARTS

Here are the ranges of the most common keys of bawu and hulusi:

KEY OF LOW D

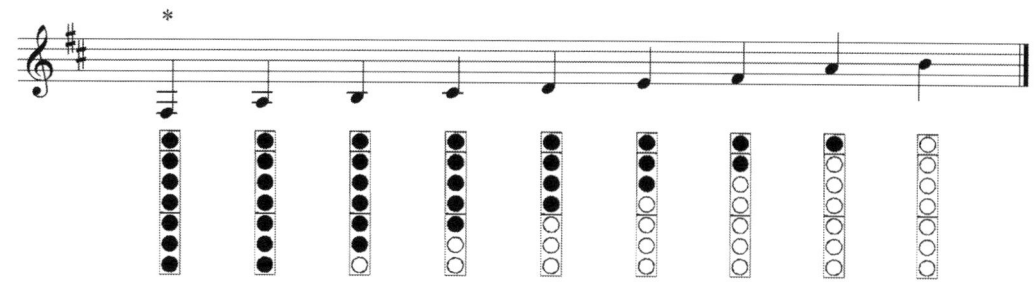

KEY OF F

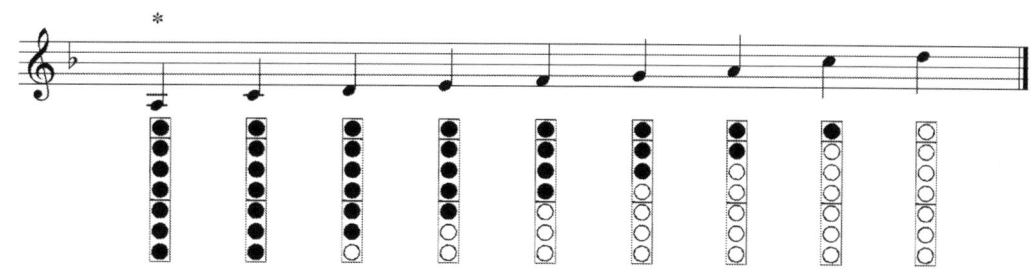

KEY OF G

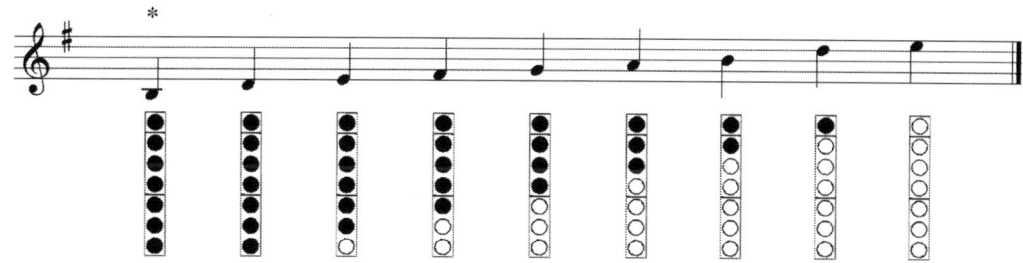

KEY OF A

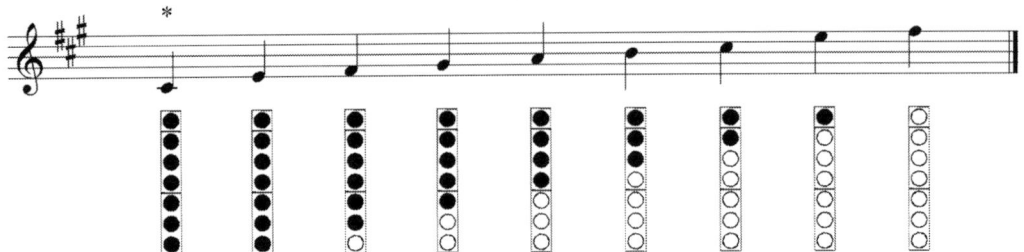

KEY OF B♭

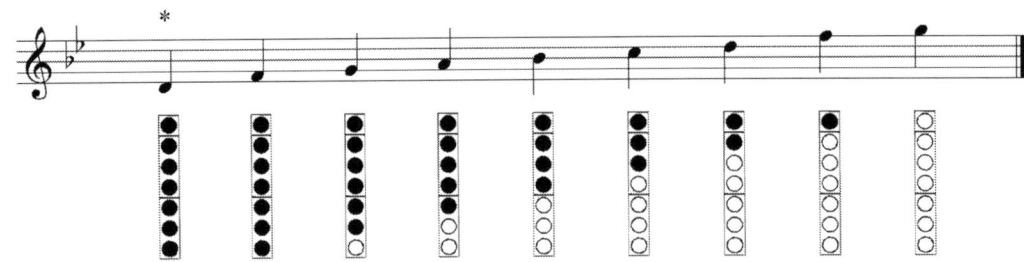

KEY OF C

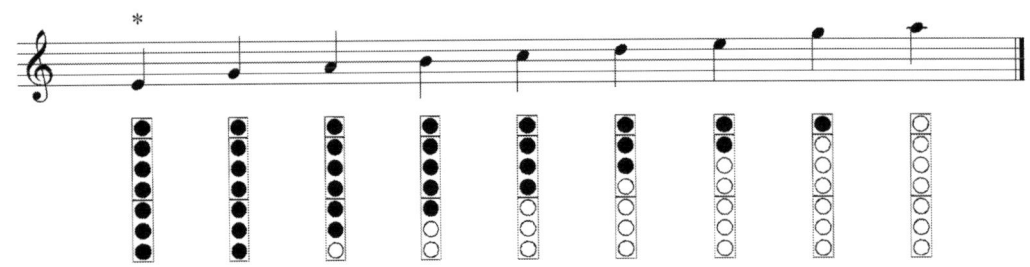

KEY OF HIGH D

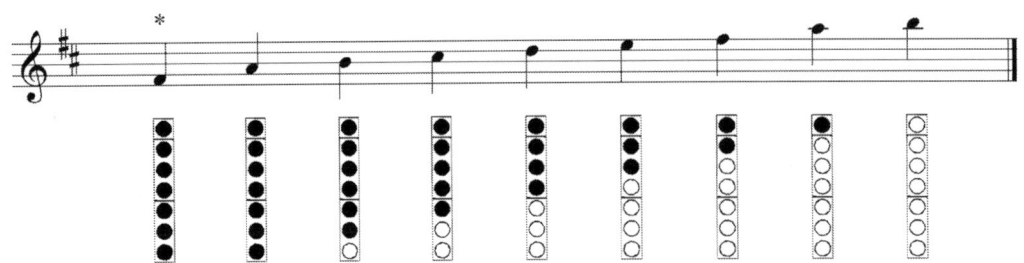

RECOMMENDED LISTENING

Over the past decade there have been a lot of CDs issued in China featuring the bawu and hulusi. Unfortunately, most of them are not readily available outside of China and they tend to go out of print so quickly that to try to list them all here would be pointless. Also, whilst the standard of the playing is usually quite high, the accompaniment often tends towards muzak. The following CDs should be considerably easier to find and although they typically only have one or two bawu or hulusi tracks per disk, the playing is of a very high standard with quality accompaniment. The individual tracks may also be available as .mp3 downloads from iTunes or amazon.com

"Yunnan Instrumental Music", Chinese Ensemble of Yunnan Song and Dance Troupe (Hugo HRP-7206)

Some great traditional music, played by gifted musicians, with excellent production. Shang Zesan plays a hulusi with double melody pipes on "Golden Peacock and Fengwei Bamboo", Zheng Quiang plays hulusi on "In the Recesses of the Bamboo" and Shang Yunlu plays bawu on "Folksong of Hani Tribe".

"Yuan", Guo Brothers & Shung Tian (Real World 62310)

Covering a wide range of music from the very traditional to the very modern, Guo Yue plays a variety of Chinese flutes, whilst Guo Yi plays the sheng mouth organ and contributes bawu to the track "Soldiers of the Long March".

"International Music Series: Music of China", Guo Yi and Guo Yue (Nouveau 43782-2)

The Guo Brothers again, this time in more traditional mode. An unaccompanied bawu is beautifully featured on the piece "Dawnbreaks".

"Dizi (The Art Of)", Lu Chun-Ling (Marco Polo 8.225939)

This album is mostly dedicated to the dizi flute, but Lu Chunling plays excellent bawu on "Dance Music Of Festival"

"China: Pipes Of The Minority Peoples", Liu Hongjun (JVC VICG-60382)

Liu Hongjun plays a variety of Chinese wind instruments, including bawu on the pieces "Xingkong Yehua" and "Nujiang Wuyu", hulusi on "Monsuono" and double pipe hulusi on "Hebian Xi Xinu".

"A Spray of Flower", Shanghai Music Conservatory (Hugo HRP-7142)

Some great music, but only one hulusi piece - "Phoenix at the Lakeshore" played by Liu Yin on a double hulusi.

"Treasury Of Chinese Musical Instruments Vol.1: Birds Adoring The Phoenix", Various Artists (China Record Co. CCD89-33)

Li Xianggeng plays a lovely rendition of "Fisherman's Song" on bawu.

"South Of The Clouds: Instrumental Music Of Yunnan Volume 2", Various Artists (Ode Record Co CD MANU 2021/22)

Something of a contrast to the other CDs mentioned here, this is a set of field recordings of local musicians in Yunnan Province. Some of the performances are rather rough and ready, but you get a good sense of how the music sounds in its natural habitat. Featured are hulusi tunes from Dai and Wa musicians on the tracks Bibantao, Lianghe Shange Diao, Mangshi Bazi Shange and Shuimian Diao.

FURTHER INFORMATION

As you have probably already discovered, there's not a whole lot of information out there about the bawu and hulusi, at least not in English. At the time of writing, this is the only English language book focusing on these instruments and very few English language websites go into any real detail about them. Not surprisingly, there is a lot of information on Chinese websites and fortunately there is a way to search for it even if you don't have Chinese language support on your computer.

To search for information about the bawu, type the following into your search engine:

巴乌

Be sure to include the symbols and punctuation as well as the numbers. This is the equivalent of searching for the Simplified Chinese characters "ba" and "wu" and should bring up thousands of results.

To search for information about the hulusi, enter the following into your search engine:

葫芦丝

This is the equivalent of entering the Simplified Chinese characters "hu", "lu" and "si".

If you don't have Chinese language support on your computer, then the text of the pages will be displayed as a series of small squares or question marks, but there still should be plenty of useful content for you. You can enter the address of any of these pages into Google Translate and have the text automatically translated in English for you, although the quality of the translation may leave a lot to be desired. If you do a video search you will find performances from players ranging from complete beginners to top professionals and an image search will bring up plenty of tunes in jianpu notation.

There are also a lot of Chinese discussion forums on the internet dedicated to the bawu and hulusi, but one good English language forum is Zhengyun Qin Guan Traditional Chinese Music Forum:

http://starvoid.proboards.com/index.cgi

This forum is about traditional Chinese music in general, but the bawu and hulusi are mentioned from time to time and the contributors seem friendly and knowledgeable.

Last, but hopefully not least, may I humbly recommend my own web site:

www.patmissin.com

My site mostly focuses on the harmonica, but there is a section on Asian free reed instruments that includes the bawu and hulusi. Also available are .mp3 downloads of all the musical examples in this book:

www.patmissin.com/downloads.html

If you have any comments or questions, please feel free to drop me a line using the contact form on my site.

BY THE SAME AUTHOR

THE BAWU AND HULUSI TUNEBOOK

ONE HUNDRED AND ONE TUNES FOR THESE POPULAR CHINESE WIND INSTRUMENTS

WESTERN TUNES FOR BAWU AND HULUSI

ONE HUNDRED AND ONE NON-CHINESE TUNES FOR THESE POPULAR CHINESE WIND INSTRUMENTS

THE HARMONIC MINOR TUNEBOOK

ONE HUNDRED AND ONE TUNES FOR THE TEN HOLE HARMONICA IN HARMONIC MINOR TUNING

THE ULTIMATE MINIATURE HARMONICA TUNEBOOK

365 TUNES FOR THE FOUR HOLE HARMONICA

Printed in Great Britain
by Amazon.co.uk, Ltd.,
Marston Gate.